STORY OF THE SILK ROAD

Zhang Yiping

Story
of the Silk Road

Translated by Jia Zongyi

CHINA
INTERCONTINENTAL
PRESS

图书在版编目(CIP)数据

丝绸之路/张一平著；贾宗谊译.－北京：五洲传播出版社，
2005.10（2009.5重印）
ISBN 978-7-5085-0832-0

I. 丝…
II. ①张… ②贾…
III. 丝绸之路－简介－英文
IV. K928.6

丝绸之路

著　　者：张一平
译　　者：贾宗谊
责任编辑：张　宏
装帧设计：田　林
出版发行：五洲传播出版社（北京海淀区莲花池东路北小马厂6号　邮编：100038）
承 印 者：北京联华宏凯印刷有限公司
开　　本：889 × 1194mm 1/16
印　　张：11
字　　数：110千字
版　　次：2005年10月第1版
印　　次：2009年5月第2次印刷
印　　数：7201-10500册
定　　价：90.00元

Contents

The Home of Silk

When ladies wear chi-pao, a close-fit woman's dress with high neck and slit skirt, they look gracefully slender and charming. When gentlemen wear Tang-zhuang, a Tang Dynasty-styled dress, they look elegant and handsome. Both Chi-pao and Tang-zhuang are made of silk, a fabric almost defined a civilization and brought fashion as well as culture, romantic vision and imagination from a remote and mystical country China to the western world and today this ancient fabric still enjoys a high degree of popularity.

The silk reaches the Western World along a long, time-honored merchant route and the Silk Road as known to the world today connects three continents of Asia, Europe and Africa, runs through China, Afghanistan, India, Iran, Iraq, Syria and Turkey, and finally stops at Rome in Italy. The Silk Road has witnessed bustling traders, carefree tourists, and devoted religious believers. During chaotic years of its history, some sections of the Silk Road were full of soldiers and refugees. Frequent trade and cultural exchange made this great route a common historic legacy for many countries and nations and brought prosperity to the people in the regions.

The culture of silkworms using mulberry leaves as well as silk reeling and weaving, are the invention of ancient Chinese people. Almost 5,000

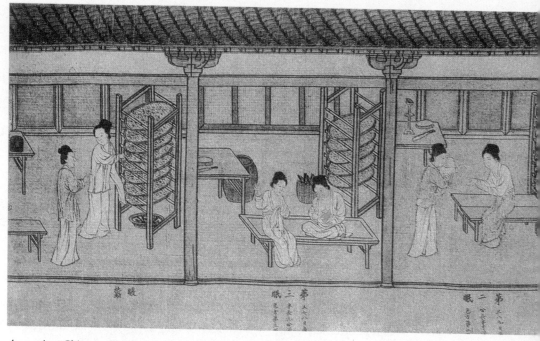

An ancient Chinese silk painting entitled "Mulberry leaves and Silkworms."

History of Suzhou Bureau of Silk Weaving, *edited by Sun Pei in Qing Dynasty. The book recorded in details the economy of Suzhou City when it was at the centre of the ancient China Silk Industry.*

A piece of ancient Chinese silk found by Stein on the Silk Road during early 20th century.

years ago, Chinese began to farm silkworm to produce silk. Archaeological discovery shows, as early as in the late Neolithic Age, residents along the Yellow River and the Yangtze River already learnt to make silk threads, ribbons and silk fabric.

There are lots of moving stories about the origin of silk. One of these tells a legendry story of silk and Yellow Emperor. More than 4,000 years ago, when a clan leader called Yellow Emperor-said to be the ancestor of the Chinese people-held a celebration, a beautiful girl came down from the heaven. She held a bundle of bright, yellow silks in one hand, and silver ones in another, and presented them to the Yellow Emperor. The ruler was delighted and ordered to make them into soft, light silk cloth. And this girl was respected as the "Goddess of silkworm."

Another story says, it was the imperial concubine of the Yellow Emperor called Lei Zu, who first discovered silk, and she taught people to grasp the art of sericulture and silk reeling and weaving. From that time on, the production of silk was gradually prospered in China.

The hieroglyphs of the silkworm, mulberry, silk and silk thread appeared in the inscriptions on bones or tortoise shells as early as in Shang Dynasty (c.16th-11th centuries BC) In the ancient tombs of Shang Dynasty also discovered jades carved with pictures of silkworms and embroidered silk fabrics. All this indicates China has mastered the technology of silk fabrication in Shang Dynasty at latest.

Whoever sees such exquisite silk dress would ask, how the silk fabric is manufactured. This is undoubtedly a marvelous process. Silk is reeled from several cocoons together. During reeling, it is very important that silk thread must not be broken. The process is similar to that silkworm makes its cocoon. Once the construction of cocoon is completed, the silkworm becomes chrysalis, which evolves into moth. The moth bites out its cocoon and flies away. Once the cocoon is open, the silk thread is broken. If it is broken, silk thread has to be repaired and spun as other fabrics. In order to keep the silk thread intact, the moth must be killed before its maturity. That is where the secret lies. Silkworm must be fed with mulberry leaves in order to make silk thread flexible and elastic as well as tenacious.

Silk fabrics have played an important role in both Eastern and Western lives from ancient times. Before Chinese silk was exported to Europe, Greece and Rome were mainly using wool and flax as raw material for their dress. As soon as the colorful, bright and soft Chinese silk cloth was introduced to Europe, the new fabric caught the imagination of local residents. Because it was expensive to produce then and the journey of Silk Road had many trade barriers and Custom duties between borders as well as the monopoly of the trade in each section of the Silk Road, silk became more valuable than gold when it reached Europe. Only a few aristocratic ladies can afford it and silk had become a symbol of high social status. Because of its huge commercial value, Europe went to a great length to acquire the knowledge of sericulture and the technology of silk manufacture. There are many stories about how the technology was introduced to Europe.

Xuanzang, a famous Chinese Buddhist monk, recorded an interesting story in his book *Da-Tang Xi-Yu Ji* (Tang Dynasty Travels in the Western Regions). In ancient time, the king of Kustana (in present Xinjiang Hotan region) learnt that the neighboring country at its east side, China had silkworm and mulberry, he sent his envoy to ask for a favor. The emperor of the eastern country not only denied the knowledge, but also ordered to implement strict border inspection to prevent the export of silkworm stocks. But this did not deter the king of Kustana and he thought out a new strategy. He wrote a flattering letter together with valuable gifts and presents to the Emperor and asked for his permission to marry his daughter. Out of an intention to cultivate a good will of the neighboring ruler, the emperor of the eastern country granted his demand. The ruler of Kustana asked his envoy to tell to the princess that he hoped her to bring some silkworm stocks with her so that he

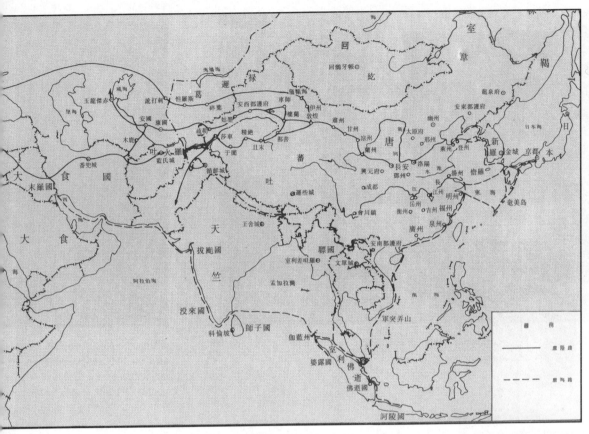

A sketch map of the Silk Road.

A legendry on how silk was brought to the west on a mural painting in ruins of Hotan Dandan Oylik site.

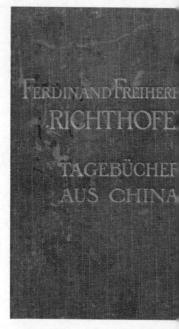

Ferdinand von Richthofen in Chinese costume and his family.

China, the Results of My Travels and the Studies Based Thereon, *by Ferdinand von Richathofen, who named "the Silk Road" for the very first time.*

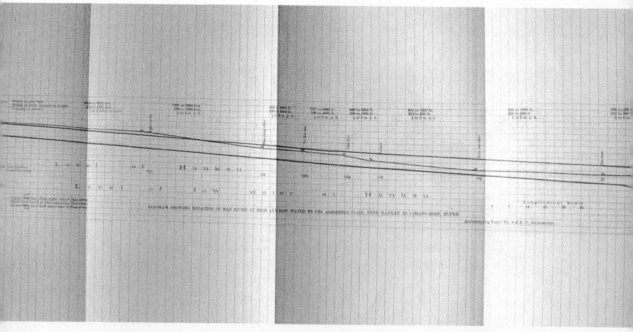

A drawing of the Silk Road by Ferdinand von Richarthofen.

could make dress with silk fabrics for her after the marriage. The princess believed him and hid silkworm stocks under her hat when she was traveling to Kustana to marry the king. The border soldiers strictly examined and checked everyone of the entourage except the princess herself. In this way, the silkworm stocks were introduced to Kustana.

Among Western scholars, ancient Greek poet Aristofen was the first to write on silk. He referred to a long frock called *Amorgia*, which was made from silk fabrics. It was around the sixth century AD that Chinese silkworm stocks and sericulture were finally introduced to Europe. Before that time, the West had no knowledge of the technique of sericulture and filature. But Europeans were able to spin raw silk imported from China or to use Chinese thin silk to produce silk thread before mixing with twine and turning into finished products. These semi-transparent silk yarns had been one of the fabrics most favored by ancient Occidentals.

It was not until AD 552 that Chinese silkworm stocks and sericulture technology were introduced to Constantinople, the capital of East Roman Empire (in the present Istanbul, Turkey). A large scale silk production started in Europe. At that time, emperor Justinian was in power. In order to break the monopoly of Persians on the silk trade, Justinian encouraged Persian merchants and Indian monks to bring the silkworm stocks and sericulture technique to Byzantium. Lots of royal silk spinning workshops arrived at Constantinople, employing a great number of working women in silk production.

Justinian monopolized the manufacture and trade of silk fabrics in East Roman Empire. Therefore, the spreading of the silk production technique was very slow in Europe. It was not until the middle of 12th Century that Italy began the production of silk fabrics, when it captured 2,000 silk spinning workers from Byzantium and moved them to the south of the country. As for Spain, France, Britain, Germany and other European countries, it was only until 13th century that they began to master the technique of silk production.

According to a report of the US *National Geography*, German archeologists discovered an ancient tomb dated 500 BC in a village near Stuttgart and identified relics of Chinese silk cloth on corpses unearthed. Chinese silk was also unearthed In Crimea, Russia. The inscriptions on other utensils, excavated at the same time, showed they were belonging to the period of 3rd century BC. These evidences indicated that silk fabrics found their way to the western world long before Zhang Qian traveled to Xiyu (Western Regions).

There are lots of ancient Greek sculptures and potteries which preserved to date with colored portraits in fine, thin, bright and transparent garments. It is estimated that, as early as in 5th century BC Chi-

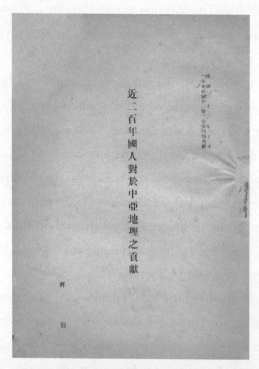

The Contribution by Chinese Scholars over Last Two Centuries to the Studies on the Central Asian Geography, *a book by Xiangbo, 1943. The book reviewed the progress made by Chinese Scholars on the Silk Road and its associated culture.*

nese silk had already become a favorite fabric for upper circles of Greece.

All of these indicate, as early as in the 2nd century BC there already was a route between Asia and Europe for exchange of goods and communication of ideas. The road was made literally by the steps of traders and nomads in wild, boundless desert and wastelands. Today the exact location of this route is not clear but we can draw an outline of this ancient route on the basis of archaeological research. It is certain that this early route had paved the way for the later Silk Road.

Zhang Qian's Journey to the West

Although the route connecting the East and the West existed before Chinese Han Dynasty it was difficult to travel and the passage on this route was often interrupted by disputes and wars between different countries and nations. No security and safety were guaranteed. It was until the time of Zhang Qian that the route prospered mainly because of the effective measures adopted by the government of Chinese Han Dynasty when it established friendly relations with the countries beyond the Pamirs.

Chinese economy prospered in Han Dynasty and sericulture in particular was well developed. The economic boom stimulated the growth of population. The Han people began to expand southward. They crossed the Yangtze River and assimilated the aboriginal tribes during the process. They gradually moved into and developed the Pearl River Valley. However, in the north, the migration of Han people stopped at the Great Wall and they could not go beyond as the Hun (Hsiung-nu) tribes often made inroad into the Han territory and presented a dangerous challenge to the Han people.

Hun was an ancient nomad nationality. At that time, they occupied

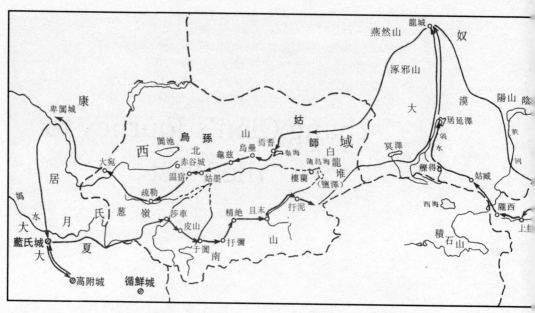

A sketch map illustrating the road taken by envoy Zhang Qian during his journey to the west.

Mongolian Plateau, boasting of hundreds of thousands cavalries. They not only seized Dayuezhi and conquered dozens of small countries in the Western Regions, including Lolan, but also frequently attacked foreign traders and travelers in the region. It had seriously hindered the East-West traffic and transportation.

During its early period, Han Dynasty was no match for Hun. The army of Hun once even besieged Liu Bang, the founder of Han Dynasty. This humiliation was engraved deeply in the minds of the Han emperors, who vowed to revenge against the enemy. After more than 60 years of vigorous efforts, China became very strong militarily. When Wudi was on the throne of the Empire, the Han Dynasty entered a period of great prosperity with a powerful army. From the first day of his rule, Wudi was determined to take large-scale military action against Hun.

Just at the time of his military preparation, Wudi got an important piece of intelligence that Chanyu (the honorable title for the chief of Hun had killed the king of Dayuezhi and humiliated the nation by using his skull to drink wine. The succeeding king of Dayuezhi was very angry at what Chanyu had done to the dead king and made up his mind to get even with the hated enemy.

Han Emperor Wu took the information very serious and he thought, "If we can make an alliance with Dayuezhi, we would cut off the right arm of Hun and put it into a position of being attacked from both sides. In this way, we are more certain to win the war against Hun." In order to implement this far-reaching military strategy of entering into an alliance with Dayuezhi, Wudi dispatched a group of more than 100 messengers, headed by Zhang Qian, to this neighboring kingdom in the period of 140-134 BC.

Zhang Qian formerly served as one of the heads of royal guard in the imperial court. Historic records said he was as robust as an ox, versed in the art of leadership and was well informed of Hun and Western Regions. His entourage included junior officers, soldiers and porters. Among them there was a man from Hun, called Ganfu. He was captured in a war by Han army. He hated the cruel Hun ruler and joined Han army. He became a loyal assistant to Zhang Qian. This group of volunteers led by Zhang Qian abandoned their comfortable life and set forth on a dangerous mission into unknown.

In the year of 138 BC the messengers set out from Chang'an (present-day Xi'an) in Northern China. Zhang Qian held a bamboo pole of 3 meters length with 3 bundles of ox hair, which served as a credential of royal representatives. He bid farewell to the Emperor and led the convoy into the unknown. They traveled hundreds of miles through the western part of Gansu, crossed the Yellow River with as little noise as possible.

They acted according to the plan of Han Emperor Wu, concealed themselves by day and marched by night, prepared to pass the Hun region and directly reach the Kingdom of Dayuezhi. However, they got astray in the desert, and unexpectedly came across a large unit of Hun soldiers.

They were captured and brought to the Chanyu of Hun. The ruler tortured the Han messengers. Zhang Qian was first put in prison. Afterwards, he was handed over to an aristocrat to serve as a slave, shepherding flocks and herds. For 11 years Zhang Qain led a slave life. He married a Hun woman slave, who had several children with him. However, he always kept in mind his mission.

Eventually, he got an opportunity to run away with his subordinates from his capturers. They continued to go westward, enduring all the hardships of an arduous journey with little food. They had to kill wild animals to allay their hunger. Sometimes they lost their direction and Zhang Qian had to judge the directions on the basis of the stars of heaven. They encountered untold difficulties and hazards before they saw a very large salt-water lake, which was situated at the present Lop Nor in Xinjiang.

Just by the lake was the capital of a country called Lolan. There was Hun army, stationed in the country. The convoy dared not to enter into it and just took rest by the lake. They inquired about the whereabouts of Dayuezhi and continued their trek along the northern edge of Tarim Basin.

At that time, there were dozens of small regimes in the region. In some places, an oasis accommodated a country in isolation. Zhang Qian and his company traveled through 8 countries, including Kizil (the present eastern suburb of Kuqa County in Xinjiang), climbed over mountains, and arrived at Dawan, a country with a population of 200,000 (in present Uzbekstan). The king of Dawan had long admired the affluence and civilization of Han Dynasty. Therefore, he was very friendly to Zhang Qian and his company. Zhang Qian had carrots, garlic and sesames for the first time, which were not available in Han territory. He also came across very strong horses, and exotic plants of garlic and grape, which he never saw in his motherland. The king of Dawan ordered his men to escort Zhang Qian and his company to the kingdom of Kangju, which in turn escorted them to Dayuezhi, the country they set to reach many years ago. Zhang Qian thought to himself that he had accomplished his mission at long last.

However, he found the king of Dayuezhi was dejected and had no ambition to revenge against the Hun. In Dayuezhi the land was fertile and its people enjoyed a good and prosperous life. The king was afraid of Hun and had no intention of fighting against it. Zhang Qian had no choice but to leave Dayuezhi for Daxia.

He stayed in Daxia for one year, making a comprehensive exploration of the places they went through. Unfortunately, on his way home, he was again captured by Hun and had to do slave labor for more than a year.

He thought, he was sure to die in this faraway alien land and would never see China again. But the fortune came to his way eventually and the aged Hun Chanyu died in 126 BC The prince and his younger brother scrabbled for the throne, resulting in a civil war. Zhang Qian seized the opportunity and escaped from Hun with his wife and Ganfu. He left Chang'an on a diplomatic mission with more than 100 men for 13 years and returned the capital of Han Dynasty with only 2 men remaining: One was himself and the other was Ganfu.

In the intervening years, despite various difficulties and dangers, Zhang Qian always carefully kept the bamboo rod with ox hairs... the symbol of royal credential. When Zhang Qian handed the bamboo rod to Han Emperor Wu, the latter was deeply moved.

Although Zhang Qian hadn't succeeded in his diplomatic mission, Wudi was fully aware of the importance of his travel. The government of Han Dynasty benefited tremendously from various data and information Zhang Qian gathered during his journey. These materials were not only related to the countries he visited, but also recorded what he saw and heard on the way. Apart from Dayuezhi, there were Dawan,

Daxia, Kangju and several other important countries, such as Parthia (Persia, the present Iran), which Han Dynasty knew very little previously

In 115 BC Wudi once more organized a convoy of 300 men, also headed by Zhang Qian, to visit the country of Wusun (in present Barkash Lake Area), trying to persuade its ruler for a united war against Hun. On his journey Zhang Qian also dispatched his assistants to the countries of Dawan, Kangju, Daxia and Dayuezhi. After a year or so, these countries sent their representatives to Chang'an along with Han assistants.

Since then, Han Dynasty established official relations with the countries in the Western Regions. The exchange and communication with the Western Regions became increasingly frequent. Han Dynasty also sent messengers to Parthia (Persia), Kizil, Hindu (India), Tiaozhi (in the north-western part of the present Persian Bay) and other countries. There were many envoys and suites with credentials and silk cloths sent to visit the countries in the region. They often came across with each other on their way to different countries of their individual mission. They were well received in most host countries. Wusun even allowed the intermarriage with Han people. Among the travelers to Western Regions, there were many merchants to follow the steps of Zhang Qian and his fellow envoys and many of them even disguised as members of imperial envoys.

Zhang Qian several times traveled to Western Regions over a period of 30 years. He devoted all his life to the establishment and development of the friendly relations between China and the countries in the west region. His health was damaged extensively due to the hardship he endured during his long years of traveling. One year after his last diplomatic mission, he died of poor health. History will remember forever this brave explorer and diplomat.

From Zhang Qian's first Xiyu mission to the last years of Western Han Dynasty, the Silk Road had prospered for 140 years. The frequent economic and cultural exchange between the East and the West promoted the development of societies in the region and the spread of civilizations along this east west corridor.

Toward the last years of Western Han Dynasty, the rebellion of Wang Mang gave an opportunity for Hun to invade the territory of Han Empire and to harass the people in the Western Regions. The transportation along the Silk Road was interrupted for more than 60 years. After the establishment of Eastern Han Dynasty, the situation on the Silk Road was improved and stabilized. The Emperor Ming dispatched an army to fight the Hun and restored the route to the Western Regions. Many warriors fought fearlessly for the reopening of the Silk Road. The most famous among them was Ban Chao.

Ban Chao was a distinctive person from very early age. When he was a young man, he engaged himself as a copyist for the feudal officialdom. He always complained: "A real man should behave like a hero, and should as Zhang Qian achieve something in the Western Regions. How can I settle for being a poor man dealing with copying all my life?" In AD 73, Ban Chao eventually gave up his pen and joined the army. Before long he received an order to go to the Western Region on a diplomatic mission with 36 agile and brave warriors.

At that time, all the small countries in the Western regions were under the control of northern Hun. It was unlikely to make them get rid of Hun control simply by diplomatic means and pledge allegiance to Han Dynasty.

After he left Yumen Pass, the first leg of Ban Chao's mission was to the country of Shanshan (in the present Xinjiang). At first, the king of Shanshan was very polite and courteous to them. Before long Hun diplomatic envoy arrived. The king was afraid of the arrival of the Hun envoy and started to alienate the messengers of Han Dynasty. And then Ban Chao decided to attack Hun convoy. In a blustering night, Ban Chao and 36 warriors quietly entered the camp where Hun was stationed.

They set on fire and attacked from both sides of the camp. The men from Hun were thrown into a panic and annihilated entirely. This act made a great impact to the king of Shanshan. He himself had long been resentful to Hun's behavior. Ban Chao persuaded him to break with Hun and return to the embrace of Han Dynasty.

Soon after this episode, Ban Chao was ordered on a mission to Yutian. There was a special resident commissioner from Hun to supervise the king of Yutian. So the king dared not to come into contact with the Han representative. The Hunophile royal wizard even demanded Ban Chao to hand over his horse and to kill it. Ban Chao readily nodded agreement. When the wizard came for the horse, Ban Chao killed him instead at one stroke. This action gave a heavy blow to Hun men. Under the advice and encouragement of Ban Chao, the king killed the Hun supervisor and entered into an alliance with Han Dynasty.

Ban Chao traveled along the edge of Tarim desert from south to north, fighting bravely for more than 20 years, persuaded Shule (in present Kashgar), Kizil (in present Aksu), Shache (in present Turpan), and Yanqi (in present Bayanbulak) to enter into a new alliance and fostered a cordial relation between these nations and Han Dynasty.

In AD 91, Ban Chao together with General Dou Xian defeated northern Hun in a fiercely fought war. They captured more than 5,000 soldiers of Hun Chanyu, who himself ran away in a panic. After this battle of defeating Changyu, the majesty and power of Ban Chao was felt throughout the Western Regions.

In AD 92, Eastern Han Dynasty established again an protection government in Kizil for Xiyu (the Western Regions) and Ban Chao was appointed the first Governor. Under his efforts, more than 50 countries of the Western Regions established friendly relations with Han Dynasty. The Silk Road had once again run freely through the Tarim Basin from south to north. The trade and economic and cultural exchange was recovered between the East and the West.

Ban Chao managed the affairs of the Western Regions for nearly 30 years. He brought with him only a small team of entourage and a few soldiers. But because mainly of his courage and resourcefulness, he was victorious everywhere on his missions to the region and forced the countries of the Western Regions to pledge allegiance to Han Dynasty, thus creating a long stable and peaceful period in the Sils Road.

He also established friendly relations with Parthia (Persia) and other countries. He even dispatched messengers to Tiaozhi (in the present Syria) and Roman Empire. The reopening of the Silk Road was instrumental in strengthening the East-West business exchanges and the integration of Han people with that of the Western Region. This was one of the most prosperous periods in the history of the Silk Road.

In AD 102, at the age of 71, Ban Chao was recalled to Chang'an, the capital of Han Dynasty, and died the same year.

China and Rome:
the Mysterious Strangers

In the early days of the Silk Road, Rome Empire and Han Empire knew very little about each other. Each imagined the other was a wonderful place, an unique mysterious and romantic paradise. Romans thought, silk was made of tree fiber. Chinese thought, Romans were able to plant mulberry and farm silkworms and they even thought Romans would look just like Chinese. Therefore, they called Rome "Great Sino."

In the endless years which followed, there existed lots of legends, myths and stories between China and Roman Empire. The secret of silk-making actually was spread to Turkistan in the 5th century, to Constantinople in the 6th century and to Sicily in the 7th century.

The legends of Sères

Since the opening of the Silk Road, a great number of official messengers and merchants brought Chinese silk products endlessly to the countries of the Western Regions, Central Asia and West Asia.

The first contact with silk made by the remote Romans was not at a market or imperial court to receive envoys from the East but at a battlefield. In 53 BC, Marcus Licinius Crassus, the governor of Roman Empire's Syria Province aspired to realize the dream of the Great Emperor Alexander of conquering the whole Asia. In the summer of that year, he commanded seven Roman field armies to enter into a decisive battle with Parthia army in a place called Carrhes within the territory of Syria.

Parthia, a former province of Persian Empire, won its independence in AD 3, and was a major country, stretching across Iranian plateau. It often went into wars with Roman Empire for the control of the Silk Road. During the battle, the Roman army was ambushed by the Parthia army. Tens of thousands of Parthia soldiers like tidewater encircled 30,000 Roman soldiers. Faced with the deafening war drums and human roaring, Roman army disintegrated into chaos.

The battle lasted till noon when the Parthia suddenly unfurled their colourful ensigns. Under the bright sunshine, these army flags sent out dazzling rays of light. The fatigued Roman soldiers didn't know what it was. They were terrified and the whole front collapsed.

The Carrhes campaign ended with a total defeat for Roman army; 20,000 soldiers were killed, and more than 10,000 captured. The Roman commander-in-chief was executed by pouring melting gold into his month.

Those bright, dazzling army flags were made of Chinese silk. This episode left a deep and unforgettable experience for the Romans. Before long, the Roman Empire tried to get Chinese silk which was far better in quality than local cotton-wool textile. 10 years after the Carrhes campaign, at one grand celebration ceremony in Rome, the Great Emperor Caesar displayed silk he acquired to the citizens of Roman. Soon after the event, silk dress became a fashion necessity for the rich and powerful in the capital.

Towards AD 14, during the last year of Augustus rule, the price of silk was equal to that of gold. Great demand in silk drained the gold reserve of Rome Empire. The senate decreed to ban all men to wear silk dress but without any success. Even special silk shops were opened in Rome to sell nothing but silk products. Gradually, the silk cloth spread to the reach of common people.

At that time, Romans knew nothing about China. Ignorance gave birth to various imagination and legendry stories. Romans called Chinese silk as the "textile from the country of Sères." The word Sères was initiated by a Greek writer, meaning the "Land of the Sères." He said, the people of Sères lived to the eastern edge of territory conquered by Alexander, where no Westerners had set foot on.

During the same time Greece and Rome had achieved a high level of civilization, and produced many great politicians, philosophers, writers and artists. The Roman Empire also boasted of a most powerful army in the world. Its navigation technology was first-class in the world. If they loved silk so much why didn't they set to sail to explore a direct route to China?

There were two obstacles standing in the way between the East and the West. One was the great number of pirates, raiding merchant boats in the Mediterranean. Pompey, one of the great politicians and strategists in the Roman Empire, led a powerful fleet to try to defeat and eradicate pirate boats in western Mediterranean Sea. During his campaign, He destroyed 1,300 pirate ships and captured more pirates than his 400 warships could carry. More than 20,000 were actually captured and further more than 10,000 pirates were thrown into sea. However, Pompey couldn't eliminate the pirate activity in the Mediterranean completely and they kept attacking merchant ships in the water for many years to come.

The other cause impeding the direct route to China was the great profits of transit trade for Parthia (Persia). Parthia maintained a friendly

Florence in Medieval Age.

relation with China, while remaining in a hostile posture with Rome. Therefore, it was reluctant to let China do direct trade with Rome at the expense of its interest.

Owing to the great profits of silk trade, merchants had deep interests in the Orient. There was no lack of adventurers who explored the possibility of going to the East both by sea and by land. The monsoon was favorable for merchant boats to cross over the Indian Ocean. They increasingly made use of the assistance of ocean wind direction to go to India, buying Chinese silk. And they learnt a great more about China during the process.

Europeans found the Silk Road by sea. The first Roman messenger went to China actually used the sea passage. There were also messengers, who tried to reach China by land. According to a book by geographer Ptolémée in AD 140, at the end of the 1st century, Maès Titianos, a

Greek merchant, organized an investigation to China by land and the exploration lasted for 7 months.

Rome in the eyes of Han Dynasty

When Zhang Qian visited the Western Regions for the first time, he had watched the performances of magicians in royal palaces. Hosts told him, the magicians came from Tiaozhi (in the present Syria) and Liqian (Rome). Zhang Qian reported what he had seen to Han Emperor Wu, who displayed much interest.

The king of Parthia learnt the keen interest of Wudi. He presented some big Tiaozhi bird eggs and several Liqian magicians to the Emperor as gifts. The magicians performed for the Han Emperor, swallowing sword and vomiting fire. Wudi was very delighted and rewarded the Parthia representatives. The magicians stayed in the royal palace and did not return. Those were the first Romans who came to China.

At that time, Han Dynasty was very prosperous. It was a most ambitious age for the Chinese people. After Eastern Han exercised control over the Western Regions, Ban Chao aspired to explore further to the mysterious country at the place where the sun set.

In AD 97, Gan Ying, the assistant to Ban Chao, was ordered to make further expedition westward from Xiyu. The destination this time was Roman Empire. Gan Ying made an arduous journey, traveling over mountains and through rivers, and came to a boundless ocean. It was the Mediterranean Sea. The sailors of Parthia told Gan Ying, "If we sail with the wind, it takes 3 months to reach the other side of the water; if the wind is unfavorable, it would take 2 years to arrive at the destination. When sailing on the sea, it is prone to be homesick and we often face with dangers and death." Gan Ying was a brace and indomitable explorer by land, but facing with the sea, he was discouraged. He turned to set foot on the journey home. Thus, the direct exchange between the East and the West was postponed for more than 1,000 years.

However Gan Ying was a hero back home, who made the farthermost travel westward in Han Dynasty. Thanks to his expedition, Han Dynasty had a wider and deeper understanding of the Western World.

According to ancient Roman documents, Rome's knowledge about China remained at the legend level of "Sères." It was natural that no official messenger was dispatched to China. However, according to *Houhan-shu* (History of Eastern Han Dynasty), in AD 166, a Roman messenger arrived in Luoyang City. He was dispatched by Roman Emperor Antonin Le Pieux. He traveled to China via Vietnam from the Indian Ocean. He offered some Roman treasures as gifts to the Emperor of Han Dynasty. But those were very common objects in the eyes of the emperor and it seemed that Chinese did not pay much attention to Europe's first diplomatic action to the Orient.

The messenger indicated that the Roman emperor hoped to establish trade relations with China. He made a detailed introduction of Rome. In this way, Chinese had a much clearer understanding of Rome.

The *Hou-han-shu* gave a vivid description of Roman Empire. It said, the Great Sino, or Lijian, was a "country at the west side of the sea." It had a territory of thousands of kilometers and more than 400 cities. Cities were walled with stones, and lined with posts. The capital had 5 palaces with crystal columns. It also wrote about the political systems of Rome. The Han people appreciated the parliament and election in Rome but did not understand how the Emperor could rule without absolute power.

When the East and the West interacted, Chinese made more and more contacts with Romans. This was a good opportunity to communicate with each other. If the spirit of travel experienced by Zhang Qian and other pioneers continued and the Silk Road extended to Rome, how would the world look like today? But China lost such an opportunity.

Several decades later, the corruption of Eastern Han government led to more than 300 years of disruption and wars. The Silk Road was interrupted again. It is not until prosperous Tang Dynasty that the Silk Road recovered its importance as an international trade route.

Tribes on China's Western Frontier During Han Dynasty

Several years before the death of Zhang Qian, the emperor of Han Dynasty was most interested in Daxia (Baketria), always thinking of opening a trade route with Daxia from south. Previous efforts had been made to export commodities via Sichuan. Unfortunately, they failed to reach their destination because of the obstruction by savage tribes in mountainous areas. Wudi couldn't but dispatch groups of messengers along the familiar roads, trodden by Zhang Qian in the north-west regions, to bring gifts to the rulers of small countries, who in turn gave "articles of tribute" to the Han Emperor as a symbol of friendship to acknowledge allegiance to Han Dynasty. The Han Emperor Wu continually expanded the territory. He conquered the Hun and received the articles of tribute from the Western Regions. Historians compared Wudi to Louis XIV of France.

An ancient desert country – Lolan

It is impossible to ascertain when the country of Lolan was

Ruins of the Ancient City Loulan unearthed at the beginning of 20th century.

established. But according to the records of that time, in the early period of Western Han, Lolan was an important oasis on the Silk Road.

Although with only a sparse population, ancient Lolan was abounding in natural wealth and rich in water resources. Strategically situated on a route connecting the East and the West, it played an important role in Han Dynasty's conquering the Hun and exploiting the Western Regions. However, in around 4th century, this prosperous ancient country of Lolan suddenly disappeared from the earth, leaving behind numerous intricate and confusing legends. From then on, Lolan becomes a mysterious place in the Lop Nor wildness.

In order to reveal the secret of the disappeared Lolan, it is important to review the history how the Silk Road was established in Han Dynasty. After Zhang Qian had traveled the Western Regions, Wudi adopted a series of policies and measures to manage and control the Silk Road and the countries along it. Owing to its strategic position, Lolan became the first target for Han Dynasty to conquer. Wudi dispatched lots of missions to contact Dawan, Lolan and others, but these countries were controlled by Hun and the envoys were attacked by Hun soldiers. Wudi couldn't tolerate this and instructed Zhao Ponu to attack Gushi and Lolan. Zhao Ponu led only 700 cavalrymen and captured the king of Lolan. The Hun wouldn't resign to this situation. It sent an army to regain Lolan. Lolan dared not offend Hun. So the king of Lolan sent one of his sons to Hun and another son to Han Dynasty as hostages. Wudi was angry and arrested the king of Lolan again, who was brought to Chang'an. Wudi questioned him. He answered, "We are a small country, sandwiched between two major powers. We can't but ingratiate ourselves with both of you. If you like I would move our country within the territory of Han Dynasty." Wudi felt the king of Lolan was telling the truth and set him free.

The national strength of Han Dynasty was increasingly enhanced and it exercised effective control of Lolan. Under these circumstances, the trade and cultural exchanges along the Silk Road increased a great deal. The early Silk Road run westward through Hexi (Gansu) Corridor, out of Dunhuang, and stopped at Lolan dividing into two directions - one leading toward Yanqi, Kizil, Shule in the northwest and the other toward Charkhlik, Yutian in the southwest. Messengers and merchants from Dayuezhi, Parthia, Dawan, Wusun and Kangju took rest here and replenished fresh supply. It is not difficult to imagine how lively and prosperous was Lolan at its heyday.

However, conditions changed all at once. As soon as the king of Lolan died, the prince who went to Hun as a hostage came back to succeed the throne in Lolan. Lolan alienated the Han Dynasty and submitted to Hun again. Han Dynasty couldn't sit idle at this turnabout. In 77 BC the Han government took resolute measures, killed the newly-enthroned king, and supported pro-Han prince Wei Tuqi to the throne. Lolan was renamed as Shanshan.

From this time, Shanshan replaced Lolan in history records. And many changes followed. The Han army started to station in Lolan and it moved its capital to the city of Qianni (in the present Charkhlik area). But it never recovered the prosperity of the former Lolan. When Xuanzang of Tang Dynasty went westward for Buddhist Scriptures and passed through Lolan, it had already become a wasteland.

A country of "heavenly horses" – Wusun

From 121 to 116 BC owing to war effort against Hun, Han Dynasty lost more than 20,000 horses and therefore, it urgently needed to replenish war-horses.

Han Dynasty was an era when horses were treasured by Imperial army. There is no lack of horse stories in historic documents. In 1969, in Wuwei-a place of strategic importance in Han and Tang dynasties, copper carts with tomb figures of horses were excavated from a tomb of an Eastern Han General. One of the copper horses galloped with three hoofs raising high in the air and one tramping on a flying swallow, which gives a rich imagination of running at lightning speed.

"Heavenly horse" was a laudatory title for the excellent horses in the Western Regions. The title began with the opening of the Silk Road, when the ambitious Han Emperor Wu, out of concerns for containing the Hun, energetically developed the cavalry. Therefore, he earnestly hoped to get good horses. Once, Wudi even to resort to draw lots of consult oracles in order to acquire the best horses available. The divination said, "The divine horse comes from northwest." Then soldiers were sent by Wudi to the northwest to search for good horses in the Western Regions. At that time, Wusun was a country with a population of 630,000 but an army of 188,800. It was a major power in the region and courageous enough to stand up to the Hun and to flight against them as an equal. Zhang Qian advised Wudi to make alliance with Wusun as a counterweight to the Hun. The emperor consented to the advice. Zhang Qian led a mission of 300 with a great amount of valuables to Wusun. The ruler of Wusun readily accepted the gifts from Han Dynasty and reciprocated with tens of excellent horses. Wudi gladly called these steeds "divine horses."

Hun also lassoed Wusun. On hearing that Wusun established friendly relations with Han Dynasty, the Hun ruler threatened to attack Wusun. In order to deal with the threat, Kunmo, the king of Wusun, asked Wudi for him to marry a Han prince, so as to establish a relationship of brotherhood. Wudi consulted his ministers and answered "yes." The Wusun ruler delivered thousands of excellent horses as a betrothal gift. Wudi was delighted and married a prince to Kunmo.

Although Wudi got a large number of Wusun good horses, he never stopped searching for many more and better horses in the Western Regions. When he learnt of Dawan "treasure horse" which was far better than Wusun horse. He dispatched a team of messengers with a large amount of gold to buy his dream horses. However, the king of Dawan refused to sell his horses and even killed Han representatives and robbed their treasures.

Han Emperor Wu was ablaze with anger and ordered a crusade against Dawan. General Li commanded an army of 100,000 and fought a 4-year-long war against Dawan. The war ended with a decisive victory for Han Dynasty. A new pro-Han king was enthroned in Dawan. Han army brought back 3,000 "treasure horses" and collected a great quantity of grape and clover seeds. The arrival of "treasure horses" strengthened Han armed forces, resulting in the establishment of a strong and valiant cavalry.

Dawan horse was tall and robust, better than Wusun horse. Wudi renamed Wusun horses as "west-end horse," and called its counterparts from Dawan as "heavenly horse." He even wrote a poem:

The heavenly horse comes from the West-end;
The clever and mighty conquers the vicious.

City ruins in Lop Nor.

It travels tens of thousands miles to the virtuous;
We cross over mountains and rivers to subjugate wild tribes.

The story about "heavenly horse" spread far and wide in the empire and beyond. The king of Dawan offered two "heavenly horses" to Han government each year and developed very close and friendly relations with Han Dynasty.

Mysterious oasis – Niya

To the southern end of Taklamakan Desert there had been an oasis, through which the Niya River quietly flew from the Kunlun Mountains. By the River lived the ancient people of the kingdom of Jingjue. The dense forests along the river as if told the prosperity of those years.

A lost civilisation in desert: Niya Site.

According the history book *Han-shu* (History of Western Han Dynasty), Jingjue was a small country of a population of only 3360 and an army of 500. In the early period of Eastern Han Dynasty, Jingjue and other small countries was annexed by Shanshan. These once prosperous small countries gradually went on the decline and fell into decay. For the country of Jingjue in the depth of Takla Makan Desert, the greater threat was the deteriorating of environment. The irrigation system became ineffective; the quicksand ran rampant; and the original oasis disappeared altogether. Jingjue faced a severe test for its survival. Just as Lolan, Niya and Jingjue were both destined to the extinction.

In January 1901, Stein for the first time made an exploration to the territory of Hotan along the southern section of the Silk Road and discovered ruins of an ancient city. He excavated the building sites and found lots of valuable relics. The unearthed cultural relics showed, the country of Jingjue experienced a long period of prosperity. It was enriched by the influences of both Eastern and Western culture as trade exchanges of the Silk Road. It had many magnificent buildings with fine sculptures. Some of the inscribed wooden slips with Chinese characters were related to land business contracts, which indicated the strong impact of Han Culture and reflected the effective control from the central Chinese authority over the administrative affairs in this area.

The country of "dance accompanied by music" – Kizil

Kizil was situated between the Tianshan Mountain and Takla Makan Desert and it was an important trade center of the northern section of the Silk Road. It was a stronger oasis city-state of some 36 countries existed in the Western Regions. According to *Han-shu*, it boasted of a population of 81,317 and an army of 21,076. Kizil bordered with Jingjue to the south and with Wusun to the north. Its capital was large and magnificent and it was well developed in manufacture and trade. Because of its strategically important geographic position and its national strength, Kizil became a target for Hun and Han to conquer.

In the time of Han Emperor Wu, Zhang Qian opened the Silk Road, and Wei Qing and Huo Qubing defeated the Hun army. Under these circumstances, countries in the Western Regions, including Kizil, pledged allegiance to Han Dynasty, and established close, friendly relations with Han Dynasty.

In the time of Han Emperor Xuan, the princess of Wusun sent her daughter to Chang'an to study musical instrument and the traditional Chinese culture. On her way home, the princess and her daughter were held back by the king of Kizil and proposed to marry her daughter. The Princess consented to the marriage proposal and reported the matter to Han Dynasty. The king of Kizil made his intention clear to the Princess that he would like to enter into alliance with Han Dynasty.

The culture of Kizil was characterized with distinctive features of the Western Regions. Kizil was at a point of intersection for the Eastern and Western cultures. It received the cultural influence from Central, Western and Southern Asia, which integrated with its own culture. The culture of Kizil in turn had great impact on the peripheral countries in the Western Regions.

The most characteristic Kizil culture was its "dance accompanied by music." The instruments, used in the "dance accompanied music," were mostly imported from India, Persia and Egypt, such as lute, flute, drum, copper cymbals and triton. The rhythm of its music was full of exotic touch. In the period of Sui and Tang dynasties, the culture and products of the Western Regions including the Kizil "dance accompanied by music" spread far and wide in the Chinese Empire. The "dance accompanied by music" of Kizil was integrated with the traditional Chinese music and had a positive impact on the latter.

The Early Merchants on
the Silk Road

From very early on in its development Chinese people already began primitive business activities. With the progress of human civilization, long-range trade gradually appeared. The opening of the trans-Euro-Asia Silk Road injected robust vitality into commercial exchange, and the long-distance trade developed in full swing.

In ancient times, when navigation was undeveloped, long-distance trade primarily depended on travel by road. The journey would often last for several months or years. Silk Road is just such example of a long trading route. People mainly depended on camels, horses and mules to carry their goods. A large trade convoy usually consisted of dozens or even hundreds of camels. In the heyday of Han and Tang dynasties, groups of traveling merchants and rows of commodities-carrying camels and horses came and went in an endless stream between the East and the West. The double-hump or Bactrian camels from Xinjiang and Inner Mongolia had well known for their strong carrying capabilities. They played the important role of "desert ship" in long-distance transportation over Pamirs and Iran Plateaus.

The unprecedented brisk trade brought boom and prosperity to the ancient countries and city-states along the Silk Road. In its long period of more than one thousand years, the camel caravans always were the most attractive landscape on the horizon of Silk Road in the boundless desert.

Prosperous Trade in Han Dynasty

Silk cloth was the main product, transported by trade caravans to Western Regions, and was well received by the residents in Central and Western Asia as well as in Europe. With increased silk trade, some countries in the Western Regions established transit depots, and actively took part in the silk transportation. For example, Shule (in the present Xinjiang) was an important distributing center, because it was situated at an interjunction for the southern and northern sections of the Silk Road. The people of Kangju were particularly good at trade and in crowds and groups drove camel caravans with fur coats and spices to Chang'an to swap silk products, which in turn were transported to Iran and Central Asia.

Parthia was historically a hub of exchange for goods and information on the Silk Road. It established close trade relations with Han Dynasty and controlled the silk trade between China and the West for a long time. Great Sino (Roman Empire) at the eastern bank of the Mediterranean Sea was the largest consumer of Chinese silk. In order to break Parthia's monopoly of silk transit trade, it entered into war with Parthia several times. It made efforts to try to open up new direct channels with China.

Chinese trade caravans from Chang'an to the Western Regions were a major force to export silk. The official messengers, dispatched by Han government, were in fact trading officers. They led large camel caravans with great quantities of silk fabrics, gold and flocks and herds, in their

48

The stature of ancient Greek, which was associated with many legendry stories.

official missions. They made extensive contact with the people of Dayuezhi, Persia, Greece and India. In Han dynasty, Chinese trade caravans had already reached many countries in Central, Western and Southern Asia. Their footprints were left on the Amu River Darya Valley, northern Caspian Sea, Iran Plateau, northern India, Syria, Roman Empire and countries along the Mediterranean Sea.

Han Emperor Wu was a ruler who appreciated the importance of other cultures and tried to integrate them with Chinese own culture. He built a rest palace in the suburb of Chang'an. It was a royal garden for hunting and other entertainments. Its style embodied the crystallization of Sino-foreign cultural flavors. The stone lion at the gate of the garden was sculptured according to the pattern of Parthia lion. This perhaps was the early origin of Chinese tradition using stone lion guarding at gate. On the folding screens in the palace halls were painted Indian peacocks spreading their tails. Chairs and tea tables were embedded with Hotan jades. In the palace were full of spices from India, and it displayed ostrich eggs from Parthia and crystal plates from Qiantu. In the garden planted alfalfa and grapes from Dawan.

There was a interesting story of how Rome's glue was introduced into China and gained the favor of Chinese emperor. This glue was a quality one made of bone extracts. It could glue the broken bows and swords. At first, Wudi would not believe in the power it had. One day, Wudi went hunting in forests. His bowstring broke and the glue at last had its opportunity to show its function. Wudi liked its strong sticking ability and it since then become an important item in the imperial court.

At that time, lots of Xiyu products were exported to Chang'an, such as sesame, figs, pomegranate, mung bean, cucumber, scallion, carrot, garlic, crocus, coriander, rattan, glass, woolen cloth, gem and medicament. Gansu served as a corridor for the products to spread to the hinterland and benefited a great deal from the international and national exchanges. For thousands of years, Gansu planted benne, horsebean, legumina, carrot, shallot, garlic and walnut, all of which originated from the Western Regions. Pomegranate first was planted around Chang'an. Afterwards, it spread to Lintong, 25 kilometers from Chang'an. Owing to its particularly favorable conditions, Lintong's pomegranate is of the best quality, becoming one of the famous Chinese products up to the present.

In the frequent trade exchanges, the highly developed Han Culture also spread to the Western Regions. Famous Chinese products, exported to Xiyu, included lacquerwork, bamboo utensils, copper cash, ginger, cinnamon, rhubarb, Tuckahoe. Of course, the most important among them were silk fabrics and iron and steel.

At that time, a considerable amount of iron and steel was exported from China to the countries in the west regions and beyond including the Kingdom of Parthia. There were two transportation routes, one along the Silk Road westward through Shaanxi, Gansu, Qinghai and Xinjiang to Parthia; the other from Sichuan via Yunnan into Burma and northern India to the eastern part of Parthia. The Mulu City in northern Parthia was a distributing center for Chinese iron and steel. Some of Chinese iron and steel were transited through Parthia to Rome and other West-

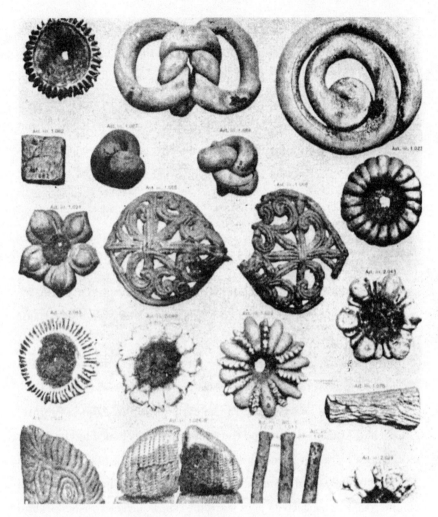

Food made of wheat unearthed on the Silk Road.

ern countries. Roman author Plinni paid a high tribute to Chinese iron and steel, calling them "excellent products."

Han metallurgy and well drill technique were also introduced to Central Asia in a similar way. Formerly, the country of Dawan didn't know the smelting and casting technology. It was Han messengers who taught them the know-how. Since then the people of Dawan was able to cast new weapons and began to improve their means of production, turning wooden plough into iron one. When Wudi attacked Dawan and the

Chinese army besieged its capital. there was no well in the city and the residents had no water supply source within the city. As Chinese soldiers effectively controlled the sources of water to the city, Dawan was forced to surrender and make peace with the Chinese army. However in this war, Dawan undoubtedly learnt from Chinese how to dig wells and they acquire the technology in a hard way. This technique was very important for the production and life in the Western Regions.

Transnational Businessmen – Greeks and Jews

For generations, Greeks were enterprising businessmen. Even up to, at present time, from Said Port to Madagascar there are many major trade firms, managed by Greeks.

In the time of Alexander the Great, all the land adventurers and navigation explorers were attracted to his side. From Marseilles to Babylon, Greeks were seen everywhere. In the early period of Roman Empire, Greeks and Romans dominated the trading markets boarding the Mediterranean Sea. Even in Rome, there were many Greek agents. They owned extravagant shops and stores in the capital. Greek became effectively a commercial language. Even Jews started to speak Greek too. Sailors and captains were mainly Greeks or Syrians. They sailed in the Mediterranean Sea, transporting Oriental products from Syrian coast and Alexander Port to Rome. And Chinese silk came on the top of the list for the merchants to transport westwards. On the return trip, they carried Italian wine and other products.

Jews were entrepreneurs and had a long history of trade and marketing. They controlled a considerable part of the trade. They played an important role in developing the economies of Mediterranean nations. The settlements of Jews were scattered almost everywhere in the Roman Empire. They left their footprints on all the continents of the world.

In Alexander Port, they monopolized the shipping. They exploited markets in Syria. They manipulated parts of the silk trade with the Far East.

Jews in Babylon learnt textile process. Jerusalem and Alexander soon became major textile centers for Jews. Beirut was center for Jew Silk workers. As for printing and dyeing, it was also one of the very important specialties Jews mastered. In AD 2nd century, some professional silk units were consisted exclusively of Jews.

Many of Jews also specialized in the manufacture of colored glass wares. Therefore, they could use glaze artworks, especially the famous necklace beads to pay for silk products. Among Jews there were many great businessmen and bankers. They had accumulated enough moneys and wealth to be capable of developing and participating a trade over a long distance. From AD 4th century, they were increasingly engaged in the operation of various exotic products, including silk commodities from remote China.

The Introduction of Buddhism into China via the Silk Road

A fter centuries of contacts, two highly developed civilizations were inevitable to interact in various other fields than trade only. The spread of religions between Indian Kingdom and China of Han Dynasty was one of the activities which had great impacts on the history of world civilization.

Buddhism Entering China

Buddhism was founded by Sakyamuni in Nepal. He abandoned a secular life and lived in self-imposed seclusion. He came to know the essence of Buddhism that the world was a long, deciduous river, full of disaster.

When Eastern Han Kingdom in China came to the last few years of its existence, separation had replaced unity and wars and death had replaced stability and prosperity. China was plunged deep into civil wars, which lasted more than 300 years. As a consequence, China lost its interest to the outside world and its door to the outside world was closed temporarily. The bustling trade exchanges were also interrupted.

Residents in the Western Regions and remote areas kept moving to the hinterland and Hexi Corridor. Many nationalities started to live together and merged with each other. The Western ideologies and cultures gradually permeated into the hinterland of China. Buddhism was spread to China via the Silk Road and became the mainstream of ideology and culture since Wei and Jin dynasties.

It may be a historic coincidence that when Sakyamuni, the founder of Buddhism, was born in India, Confucius, the founder of Confucianism, and Lao Zi, the founder of Taoism, were born in China. In the time of Eastern Han, Confucianism started to decline after many years of dominance in the official ideology because it stopped to embrace new ideas and accommodate diversity. This provided a golden opportunity for Buddhism with its strong vitality to enter the main stream thinking of China political elite and started to dominate the ideology of China for many years to come.

The introduction of Buddhism to China began in the middle period of Eastern Han Dynasty. According to *Hou-han-shu*, Eastern Han Emperor Ming dreamed of a God, with shining golden rays all over his body flying down from the heaven. Next day, he consulted his ministers. One erudite minister answered, "It is learnt that in the West there is a God, called Buddha. It must be He that Your Majesty dreamed of." Mingdi immediately dispatched a group of officials, headed by Cai Yin, to Tenjiku (ancient India) to search for Buddhism. On the way, they met with two Masters Kasyapa-matanga and Dharma-ratna, who came from Tenjiku to China to do missionary work. Under the invitation from Cai Yin two senior monks, with white horses carrying Buddhist Scripture and the figure of Buddha on the back came to Luoyang, the capital of Eastern Han Dynasty. Mingdi welcomed the arrival of Buddhist missionary and ordered to build a temple for them which was named "White Horse Temple" in commemoration of white horses carrying Buddhist Scripture. Kasyapa-matanga and Dharma-ratna lived in the temple to translate

Buddhist story on silk roll paintings at Dunhuang Caves.

Buddhist Scripture into Chinese until their death. Today, this famous ancient temple still stands erect in the eastern suburb of Luoyang. At the gate of the temple is a stone carving of white horse. Within the temple lie the tombs of Kasyapa-matanga and Dharma-ratna, lined with the evergreen pines and cypresses.

At that time there were many other Buddhist missionary monks, who came along the Silk Road to China. The most famous among them were An Shigao, Buddhacinga and Kumarajiva.

Anshigao was the prince of Parthia. After believing in Buddhism, he detested and rejected royal secular life, and engaged in traveling as missionary monk for all of his life. In the time of Eastern Hang Xuandi, he came from Central Asia to Luoyang, the capital of Eastern Han, and settled there, devoting all his life to the translating of Buddhist Scripture. In 20 years, he had translated more than 30 volumes of Buddhist Scripture. Indian Buddhist Scripture, written in Sanskrit, was too abstruse. His translation had direct bearing on the spread of Buddhism in China. He made great contributions to the exchange of Sino-Indian religious culture and was highly respected by his disciples.

Buddhacinga was a monk from Kizil in the Western Regions. Soon after his arrival at Luoyang, a war broke. He threw himself into the lap of Shile, the leader of Jie tribe. Buddhacinga was shrewd and able person and good at performing magic. Shile was fascinated with his wizard act. Actually based on his sensitive political sense and judgment, he successfully augured the outcome of several battles with magic acts. Shile admired him very much and respectfully called him "the Great Monk."

Before long, another senior monk Kumarajiva came to China from Tenjiku. He played also a very important role in the spread of Buddhism in China. He was borne to the family of Minister. His father was an erudite Buddhist, reluctant to succeed the post of a minister and left home for Kizil in the Western Regions. The king of Kizil was a pious disciple of Buddhism and married his younger sister to the Indian Buddhist. She bore him a son. That was Kumarajiva, who became a monk at the age of 7. He extensively read the volumes of Buddhist Scripture and become a famous scholar in the country of Kizil at the age of 20. The kings in the Western Regions one by one invited him to come to their countries to preach the Buddhist Scripture. His fame spread far and wide.

One day before she returned to Tenjiku the mother of Kumarajiva asked her son: "You are already a man of great learning. It is a glorious obligation for you to spread Buddhism to the east. However it is an

A mural painting, discovered by Stein in ruins of the City Miran, illustrating the story of Indian Prince Vessantara.

unprofitable undertaking involving many hardships. How do you think about it?" Kumarajiva replied, "As long as I can spread the truth and justice all over the world, I can endure anything. I don't repent."

At that time, Fujian, the ruler of Qianqin, heard of the great name of Kumarajiva. He intended to invite Kumarajiv to preach Buddhism in the Kingdom. So he ordered his general Lu Guang to command an army of 70,000, attacking Kizil in AD 382. Next year, Lu Guang conquered Kizil and more than 30 small countries in the Western Regions. He captured a great amount of valuables and returned with Kumarajiva.

Kumarajiva was but a young man in his twenties. Lu Guang didn't believe in his ability and mad fun of the young man very often. Kumarajiva quietly tolerated. One day, Lu Guang's army encamped at the foot of the mountain. Kumarajiva had forecasted the arrival of forthcoming strong storm and persuaded Lu Guang to move the army upward to the top of the mountain. Lu Guang turned a deaf ear to his advice. At midnight, a rainstorm poured down, and thousands of soldiers were drowned and washed away in a major land slide. From then on, Lu Guang changed his arrogant attitude toward Kumarajiva and consulted him almost on everything.

In his late years, Kumarajiva preached Buddhist Scripture in Caotang Temple (in present Hu County, Shaanxi Province). There were 3,000 disciples receiving his teaching. In AD 409, he died in Chang'an. His body was cremated according to Indian Buddhist tradition and his ashes were kept in Caotang Temple.

Kumarajiva was a rigorous, studious monk. He was well versed in Sanskrit and Chinese. During the 8 years of his stay in Chang'an, he had translated 98 titles of Buddhist Scripture in 425 volumes. When translating, Kumarajiva held Buddhist Scripture in hand and read his Chinese version aloud. Wherever coming across difficult paragraphs, he stopped to consult disciples until found a perfect translation. His translating not only publicized Buddhist classics but also improved the

Sanskrit of Chinese scholars.

Chinese monks going westward along the Silk Road

Monks from the Western Regions came to China to preach Buddhism. They inspired generations of Chinese monks to go to the Western Regions and India for learning Buddhist Scripture for themselves. At that time, Buddhism was wide spread all over China. Temples were scattered everywhere. But original Buddhist classics were scares in the Kingdom and sought after by all the new created temples. The poor translation always led to differences in understanding. Consequently, some ambitious Chinese monks made up their minds to go to the "Western Heaven" and to bring back the true Buddhist Scripture.

According to historical records, Zhu Shixing in the period of Three Kingdoms was the first Chinese who went westward for Buddhist Scriptures. In AD 260, he reached Yutian (in the present Hotan, Xinjiang). Faxian in the period of East Jin was the first Chinese who reached India.

Faxian, born in Linfen County, in the north of China's Shanxi Province, lived in Chang'an as a monk in the early period of Houqin. At that time, Kumarajiva hadn't arrived in Chang'an. Faxian felt a lack of Buddhist Scripture. Faxian and several other monks, including Huijing, Huiying, Huiwei and Daozheng, decided to go to Tenjiku for Buddhist Scripture. In the middle of March AD 399, they left Chang'an.

They went westward through desert, experienced untold hardships and tribulations, passing through more than 30 countries, including Kashmir, Pakistan, India and Sri Lanka. When they traveled though the 5,200 meters high Sunaman Mountain, Huijing was frozen to death in a storm. He said to Faxian, "I'm dying. You must live and forge ahead."

Chinese manuscripts of Buddhist readings in Dunhuang Caves.

Faxian with tears in the eyes, determined to reach the final destination. He succeeded eventually.

Faxian lived in India for 3 years, learned Sanskrit and copies many volumes of Buddhist Scripture. Afterwards, he crossed the sea along with merchants and arrived at the so-called Lion country-Sri Lanka. He stayed there for 2 years. By that time, he was alone. All his companions died on the way or abandoned the effort and left. One day, he saw a merchant offered a white, circular Chinese fan before Buddha. The scene evoked his nostalgic feelings for the homeland. He decided to return to China.

In July AD 404, Faxian returned to Qingdao China. More than 15 years elapsed since he left Chang'an. He brought back with him many volumes of Buddhist Scriptures. Based on his own experiences, he wrote a book, entitled *Travels in Buddha Countries*, which still is an important book in the study of the Silk Road, the histories of countries in the Western Regions and India.

103 years after the return of Faxian, another monk in Dunhuang, Gansu, called Songyun, was ordered to go to the Western Regions, searching for Buddhist literature. He had the company of Huisheng. They felt Luoyang and reached Qinghai after 40 days of long and difficult journey.

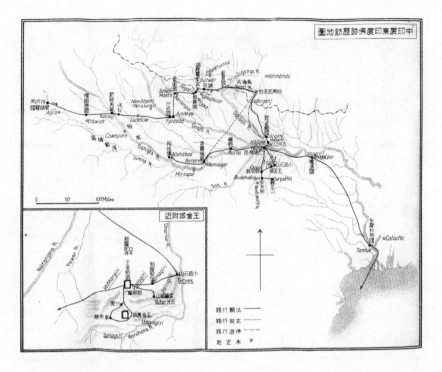

A map showing the route of monk Faxian's journey to India

Travels in Buddha Countries *by monk Faxian, an important book which has been translated into many languages in the world.*

They kept traveling to Shanshan, Yutian, and eventually entered Afghanistan and Pakistan. In AD 522, they came back to Luoyang, bringing with them 170 titles of Scripture literature and records of what they had seen and heard on the way.

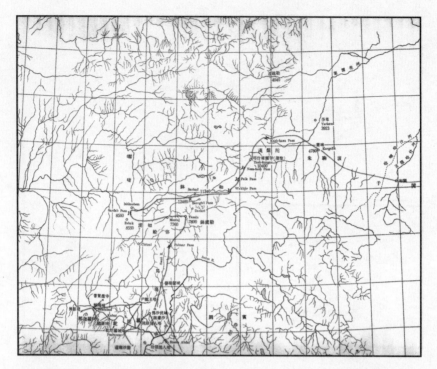

A route map of Song Yun's journey to the west, from the book Luoyang Jianlan ji.

Songyun and Huisheng had been to the capital of Uiyna, a country in the present Pakistan, visited Tuoluo Temple and the relics of Buddha. They told the king about great Chinese philosophers, such as Confucius, Zhuang Zi, Lao Zi and famous ancient doctor Hua Tuo. The king was delighted and become friendly with them. He called them "the persons, coming from the sun-rising country." He was yearning for China.

The Dispute on the West End of the Silk Road

The AD 3rd century witnessed a deep and broad upheaval sweeping across European and Asian Continents. In the west, Roman Empire suffered from serious economic crisis. The political center moved to the Mediterranean Sea. Alexander established Byzantium which replaced the position of Rome. In the east, the Han Kingdom in China was in the process of disintegration. China entered a time when many small kingdoms fought against each other.

The political upheaval in the East led to exchange between China and the Western Regions stopped and the Silk Road was interrupted almost for a century. From the beginning of AD 184, there were a lot of coup plots, which resulted in the disappearing of Han Kingdom and the establishment of Three Kingdoms. China's northern part belonged to Wei Kingdom. As a result, silk trade came to a complete standstill. A close-door situation appeared both in Roman and Chinese Empires. That is why there was a complete gap in history of exchanges between the two empires.

In the West, from around AD 270, economy began to recover. In AD 330 the capital of Roman Empire moved to Constantinople. The interest of the West in silk did not decrease. When the king of Persia conquered Syria of the Byzantine Empire, he ordered to gather Syrian silk craftsmen and specialists of spinning and weaving as well as printing and dyeing and transported them back to Susa away from Byzantium. This measure greatly promoted the development of Persian silk industry. Before that, Persian merchants were mainly to purchase the silk products from India.

The use of silk in Byzantium grew more and more popularity. When Christianity was adopted as a national religion, Christians began to wear silk costumes and churches to use silk fabrics as curtains, this created further demand for silk Afterwards, a custom using silk clothes to wrap body of VIPs when burying them was developed gradually. The silk was so important to Byzantium that the fluctuating of silk price could be a measurement of the political stability of the Byzantine Empire.

At that time however, Byzantine Empire was completely isolated from the country of Sères. In the North, the uncivilized tribes prohibited people of different races to transit the area of the Danube and the Black Sea. In the East, Persia was the greatest barrier to overcome. In the South, the Red Sea is a natural obstacle since the 2nd century, Roman boats had stopped sailing for India. The Red Sea had long been in the control of Ethiopians and Persians. Byzantium had no choice but to give up the direct trade with the East and to settle for transit trade of goods from Persians, who rapidly became the big clients for the goods from the Far East trade and also big beneficiaries of the trade. Because the northern part of China was temporarily in an isolated condition with the outside world, no Chinese businessmen were seen traveling on the Silk Road between Afghanistan and the Western Regions. From the beginning of the 4th century, the Persian ships, sailing from the coast of Mesopotamia had to cross the Red Sea for the ports in India or Ceylon and to purchase products from the southern part of China. In the period from AD 220 to 280, this new sea route was very busy. It is usually called Silk Road by sea.

Just as it was once the time of Romans, now this period was the time belonged to Persians. The Persian regime was established on the foundation of the firm and rigid feudal structure. Persia was strong and powerful. It tried every means to protect its achievements in territory conquered and take the monopoly of economic privilege. The most profitable deal was the transit trade of Chinese silk. In order to gain the cheapest price of silk, the two empires of Byzantium and Persia fought a fierce war, which lasted for more than 3 centuries.

At that time, silk was one of the important factors influencing the policies of the Byzantine Empire. Numerous historical records were found to be related to silk, such as customs regulations, peace treaty, commercial articles of association, the law on restricting luxuries and other documents. The shadow of silk even extended into the religious prayers. Bishops often uncovered fraudulent practices related to silk trades. The emperor of Byzantium adopted a economic policy to have more strict control of the silk trade. This was an ominous vicious cycle and the trade become more difficult to control. A tremendous Byzantine army fought with the Persians and the uncivilized tribes for the control of the silk trade. The payment for the silk drained the treasury of Byzantium. In order to enrich the treasury, there was no choice but for the Empire to increase taxation and to have the monopoly of economy. The Empire replied heavily on the tax collected from the silk trade. From AD 4th century, Persian intermediate brokers effectively controlled the import of silk products.

When Byzantium felt it was powerful enough to fight a decisive battle with Sasanian Dynasty, an understanding was reached at last between them. In AD 297, emperor Diocletian and king Narses agreed to designate Nisibine as the only exchange center for silk. In fact, this was only a custom city. No other place was allowed to engage in silk business. In AD 408 and 409, Byzantium signed silk trade agreements with Sasanian

Dynasty. In AD 528, Byzantine Empire again entered into war with Persian Empire, which resulted in the interruption of the Silk Road. In order to open the commercial route to the Orient and maintain the silk trade with China, the empires of Rome and Byzantium waged wars for more than 5 centuries, until the end of Persian Empire.

The Great Tang Dynasty and the Golden Age of the Silk Road

Tang Dynasty is one of the most powerful and prosperous king doms in the history of China. Central Plains of China and the Western Regions entered into a grand unification. In the first 100 years of Tang Dynasty its prosperity allowed it to reach an unprecedented height in the exchange and communication with the outside world. Contemporary historians both in China and abroad call Tang Dynasty "an open empire" and Chang'an "a capital of the world." Traders of Persia, priests of Rome, sailors of Arabia, and students of Japan, as well as Buddhist and Islamic scholars, all of them gathered in China. Because of rapid development of its economy, China's trade exchange with the Western Regions and beyond increased a great deal during the period. A golden era in the history of the Silk Road started with the arrival of Tang Dynasty.

Buddhist paintings, brought back to France by Paul Pelliot.

Chang'an: an International Metropolis

Chang'an of Tang Dynasty was a magnificent, grand capital, and it was the largest metropolis in the world at that time and the center of Orient civilization. It attracted tens of thousands traders, tourists, scholars and followers of different religions from around the world.

As a consequence, the city of Chang'an was a masterpiece of ancient Chinese architecture. The design of the city was rectangle with an area of 81.8 square kilometers. The north-south axis was 8.4 kilometers and west-east axis 9.7 kilometers. Grand royal palace – Daming Palace stood high on the Longshou Mountain to the north of the city. Lofty Hanyuan Hall was the place, where the emperor interviewed foreign diplomatic envoys. The layout of the city was neat and balanced. The bustling and hustling downtowns, the graceful pagodas of Dayanta and Xiaoyanta, temples and shrines of various religions, picturesque Qujiang Pool, all of

them evoked the praises of the travelers who came to the city. Zhuque boulevard, the main trunk in the city, was as wide as 155 meters, in comparison the widest street in Rome was only 12 meters at that time.

The East and West Markets were two major commercial districts in Chang'an, a square of 1050 meters both in width and length, boasting of nearly 40,000 shops and stores. They resembled a world commodity fair. Foreign businessmen brought products to the markets from southern and western Asia as well as Europe, and such as jewels, ivories, pearls, tortoise-shells, rhinoceros horns, hawksbill, corals, diamonds, glassware, coats, haircloths, spices, medicines and horses were daily items traded at the markets. They in turn bought Chinese commodities, such as bullion products, bronze ware, porcelains, teas and papers and took with them on the journey home.

Some merchants from Persia and Central Asia opened and operated stores in Chang'an themselves and made big fortunes in the city. Persian businessmen were good at identifying and appraising treasures. One story told about a monk, a Persian merchant and a piece of Buddhist treasure. A monk got a piece of treasure but he didn't know what it was. He consulted a Persian merchant. The latter wanted to buy it at an expensive price. The monk asked for 100,000 in cash. The merchant said, this wasn't the right price. The monk asked for 500,000 in cash. The merchant smiled and said, "This is a piece of Buddha bone, worthy of tens of millions in cash."

Persian and Central Asian merchants were engaged in commerce not only in Chang'an but also elsewhere in China, such as Luoyang, Yangzhou, Guangzhou and many other cities. They were buying and selling jewelries and also operating financial institutions such as banks and pawnshops.

In the time of Tang Dynasty, Chang'an had 12 city Gates. The Kaiyuan Gate in the western city was considered to be the starting point of the Silk Road. The guests from the Western Regions entered Chang'an through this gate. At that time, Tang Kingdom had close, friendly relations with more than 70 countries.

When Tang Emperor Gaozong died, many chiefs and their representatives of minority nationalities in the Western Regions attended his funeral. In order to commemorate the event, the famous empress Wu Zetian ordered to carve stone figures of the envoys, which were laid in front of Gaozong mausoleum. On the back of the stone figures were carved the names and identities of the envoys. Thousand years elapsed and the relics of the 61 stone sculptures remain where they were.

In Tang Dynasty, the prosperity of the Silk Road promoted the exchanges of art and culture. The people in Central Asia were skilled in singing and dancing. The music of the Western Regions was famous for its beautiful and exquisite melody. When Tang emperor Taizong conquered Gaochang in the Western Regions, he ordered to bring an entire Gaochang band back to Chang'an. In Tang royal palace frequently played ten musical compositions, half of which were from Kizil, Shule, Gaochang and other countries in the Western Regions.

The increased Sino-foreign exchange in Chang'an was directly re-

Merchants travelling in endless desert.

lated to the liberal policy adopted by Tang Dynasty. Tang Emperor Taizong himself was a hybrid of Han and Xianbei nationalities. He adopted an all-embracing attitude to foreign cultures. He respected Chinese orthodoxy, but at the same time didn't exclude and reject foreign things. It was just due to the exchange and integration of different national cultures that traditional Chinese culture developed to its bright climax.

The Great Wall viewed from an observation tower near Dunhuang by Stein.

During the period of Tang Dynasty, most of the world commodities can be found in Chang'an; musical compositions and dances from different countries were performed; monks and believers of diverse religions coexisted peacefully in this capital. The features of international metropolis made Chang'an attractive to peoples from far away. Especially, Japan in the Orient sent a great numbers of students to study in China each year. Nara, the ancient Japanese capital, was constructed according to the pattern of Chang'an. Japanese characters were derived from the cursive scripts of Tang Dynasty. Even today, Japan's national costumes and festival celebrations preserved the relics of Tang Dynasty.

Dunhuang: A Metropolis of Sino-foreign Integration

Hexi Corridor was a famous route from ancient China's northern-western continent to the rest of Asia and Europe. It was a battlefield to guard and protect the Silk Road 2,000 years ago. Here happened many heroic historic events. After having won its wars against Hun, Han Dynasty instituted four counties in the Hexi Corridor from 121 BC to 111 BC They were: Wuwei, Zhangye, Jiuquan and Dunhuang.

Dunhuang, situated at the western part of the Hexi Rorridor, was a strategically important city and a hub of international trade. It was a interjunction to the northern and southern section of the Silk Road. The Western Regions, Tutian and Kizil in particular, were deeply influenced by Indian Buddhist culture. Dunhuang, as the gate to the Western Regions, was the first to receive the Indian influence and became one of China's early Buddhism centers. In Dunhuang there were many Buddhist temples. In Tang Dynasty, there were at least 16 grand Budhist temples in the city of Dunhuang with a total of more than 900 monks.

Buddhists not only built temples, but also excavated caverns, molding the figures of Buddha and drawing mural paintings on the cave walls. They were many craftsmen, officials and devotees to Buddha, who spent their life to created the art of Dunhuang. In this way, the Dunhuang Buddhist arts were gradually took its current shape. Dunhuang was also the center of translating the China's early Buddhist literature. The scholars of Buddhism translated numerous Buddhism classics. In AD 1899, in Dunhaung Thousand-Buddha Caves discovered more than 30,000 volumes of ancient books, hand-copied or block-printed, most of them were Buddhist classics. Dunhuang, as a city of international culture exchange, also in their mural paintings recorded Chinese and visitors interacting in their ordinary daily life. For example, during the period of Three Kingdom, it was a fashion for women in Dunhuang wear Indian-styled costumes.

Desert is spacious, boundless and monotonous, but 10 kilometers to the south of Dunhuang there is a place called Singing Sand Mountain. It is a place full of fascinating natural phenomena: When the wind is blowing, the Mountain sends out the sound of roaring thunder. Ancient people were surprised at this phenomenon and called it the Divine Sand Mountain. In the Mountain there is a Crescent Fountain. Thousand years elapsed, but the Singing Sand Mountain is still staying where it was. Each year at the Dragon Boat Festival on the fifth day of the fifth lunar month, boys and girls in the city of Dunhuang go in groups to the Singing Sand Mountain and the Crescent Fountain.

International Trade during Tang Dynasty

The silk trade in Tang Dynasty was prospering and reached an unprecedented level. At that time, the major trading centers were Chang'an, Luoyang, the Hexi Corridor, Yutian, Kizil, Shule, Shanshan and Turpan. In order to guarantee the peaceful trade along the Silk Road and strengthen the supervision over the West Regions, Tang Dynasty established courier stations along the main roads from Chang'an to major cities of the Western Regions. The courier stations provided food and shelter for traveling traders and messengers.

Tang Dynasty also implemented a registration system. All travelers had to register their names, ages and belongings and they would be issued a pass, without which they were not allowed to travel. The traders had to pay a certain amount of taxes for the privilege of the road pass. At major towns and strategic points were stationed army to guarantee the safety and security of passage on the Silk Road.

The government officials were allowed to use gold and silk to swap the Western Regions' horses, mules, camels, hides, woolen products, gems, jades, corals, colored glazes, medicaments and spices. Private merchants also could do business under the authorization of the government. According to the estimates of scholars in the west, in the heyday of Tang Dynasty, the volumes of Sino-foreign trade through the Silk Road amounted to one million pounds. The Chinese products exported were silk fabrics, lacquerworks, ironware, bullion and medicinal materials.

Camel, the so-called "boat in the desert," was the pillar for trade caravans. Camel is meek and docile in nature, able to endure hardships under every dry condition. It has a special sense to source water. Wherever is water, it will find it and always stops where there is potential of water under desert. People would dig where camel stops and get water supply. Camel has a weak point, and it can't endure very hot weather. That is why camel trade caravan always stops by day and travels by night.

Major trade caravan needs clever and valiant leadership. In ancient times, there were special guides and caravan heads, responsible for each section of the route from Kabul to Hotan or from Hotan to Dunhuang or Jiuquan. Some times they also acted as diplomatic envoys.

The procedures involving the trade caravans passing the toll-gates were an interesting story to read. The merchants handed relevant documents and tax certificates to the officers for examination and approval. After signing the certificate, they waved go-ahead to the merchants. When they came across important guests or major trade caravans, they had to report to the Hexi Administration for approval. The procedures were more complicated. Chinese governments of many dynasties often restricted the number of foreign traders. That was the reason why some of them tried to settle in China and became local residents.

Xinjiang was the early area to make contact and trade with the countries westwards and was an important transit station for Sino-foreign trade in ancient times. Merchants bought Chinese silk products in Xinjiang and resold them to other countries. After Zhang Qian's travel to the Western Regions, the silk fabrics flowed in an endless stream from China's hinterland to these remote areas. Chinese traders devel-

"Five Stars Rising from the East to Help China", an Eastern Han period piece unearthed at Niya site.

oped harmonic relations with local merchants.

In Yutian, Shanshan and other Xiyu cities, there were not only silk traders to and from the hinterland, but also merchants from India and Persia. Owing to its geographic position, Yutian had plenty of opportunities and economically benefited from the trade tremendously. In the period of Western Han Dynasty, Yutian had a population of only 19,000, but in the period of Eastern Han Dynasty, its population grew to more than 83,000. In the city of Yutian, temples stood in great numbers; the images of Buddha were decorated with gold. In 1930s, warlord Shen Shicai established an Administration of Gold Mine, specialized in excavating gold in ancient relics.

Hexi Corridor in Gansu was one of the transit stations and business centers for the trade between the West and the East. China's commodities were transported through Hexi and Xinjiang to Daxia, Parthia, Daqin and countries along the Mediterranean Sea. And foreign businessmen also transported their products through these places to Chang'an. In June AD 609, Shui emperor Yangdi went to Zhangye personally and interviewed messengers and merchants from 27 countries in the Western Regions.

At that time, foreign merchants often did business in Liangzhou (Wuwei), which in Tang Dynasty was a metropolis and trading center for Hexi Corridor. It is estimated that at that time Wuwei boasted of a population of 100,000.

The market in ancient Jiuquan possessed a different feature from others. It was a transit point for international trade as well as an important communication hub to the areas of minority nationalities. It preserved the ancient habits of doing business when the sun rises and to rest when the sun sets. The famous commodity in Jiuquan and Zhangye was rhubarb, which was well sold in foreign market.

Xi'ning in Qinhai was also an important international trading center. A route run from Xi'ning to Lop Nor in Xinjiang and connected with the famous southern section of the Silk Road in Xinjiang. It went westward to India. This route was once prospering with brisk business activities.

Tang Monks' Searching for True Buddhist Scriptures in Indian

Friendship Between China and India

When Zhang Qian returned from his first trip to the Western Regions and reported to the emperor what he had seen and heard there, he talked about the bamboo rod and Sichuan fabrics, transported to Daxia from Sindhu. Sendhu is the ancient India.

As early as 3,000 BC there were bronze utensils and towns in the valley of Indian River, where is regarded as one of earliest cradle of human civilization. In 1920s, archeologists successively excavated the relics of Mohenjodaro and Harappa, and revealed the ancient Indian civilization, which was neglected so far. Around 1,200 BC Aryans entered the valley of Indian River, dominated the area after a fierce war, and completed the transition from a tribe to a nation.

China and ancient India had long established friendship and cultural exchanges. As early as 5th century BC Persia trade caravans went eastward often included businessmen from Indian. Chinese silk exported to India long before the 4th century. Many ancient Indian books, such as

An Indian Buddha Stature.

On Political Affairs, mentioned Chinese silk. It is clear that Chinese silk fabrics played an important role in ancient Indian costumes and garments.

In Sino-Indian cultural exchanges, the most important is the spread of Indian Buddhism to China. It is possible that Indian Buddhism is first spreading to the countries in Central Asia, afterwards entering China via the Silk Road. Since Eastern Han Dynasty, more and more monks from Central Asia and India, such as Anshigao and Kumarajiva, went to China to translate Buddhist texts and preach Buddhism.

With the wide spread of Buddhism and the increase of its influence, Chinese monks are inspired to visit Buddhist Tenjiku (ancient India). Among them the most famous representative is Xuanzang of Tang Dynasty.

(2) Xuanzang: the pious searcher for Buddhist Scripture

Xuanzang's surname is Chen. He is born in AD 602. At the age of 13, he became a monk in Luoyang. He was an erudite, firm and persistent monk, fearless of dangers. He is also a translator and friendly envoy for Sino-foreign cultural exchanges. In the period of early Tang Dynasty, he traveled Sichaun, Hubei, Henan, Hebei and many other places, visited famous scholars and studied the Buddhist texts intensively. In his twenties, he had already achieved a high level in Buddhism research. At that time, there were divers schools of Buddhism. The lack of Buddhist classics and the improper translation of the Buddhist Scripture created lots of difficulties in the study of Buddhism. In this connection, he made up his mind to go to India, the cradle of Buddhism, to study and investigate.

In AD 627, at the age of 26, Xuanzang set out from Chang'an and began his 50,000 kilometers Xiyu pilgrimage. He went with another monk Xiaoda to Gansu. Xuanzang stayed in Liangzhou for more than one month, preaching the Scripture to local monks. More and more listeners came there from the adjacent areas. All of them praised him for his profound knowledge. The news of Xuanzang going abroad for Buddhist classics was spreading far and wide.

At that time, the road to the Western Regions was not open and the journey was full of obstacles. The authorities prohibited people going westward in fear of thei safety. The governor of Liangzhou Li Daling demanded Xuanzang returning to Chang'an. It was with the help of Hexi monk Huiwei that Xuanzang was able to continue his westward pilgrimage. However, he had to hide by day and travel by night and began his difficult journey into unknown.

Xuanzang walked 80 kilometers and came across the first beacon tower. Afraid of being discovered, he hid in the valley in daytime and went ahead at night. When he was going to fetch some water, an arrow flew down. He promptly called aloud, "I'm a monk from Chang'an. Please don't hit me." Then he went to the beacon tower and told the truth. The head of the beacon tower was a pious Buddhist. He was moved by Xuanzang's story and helped him to continue his pilgrimage.

After several months of traveling, Xuanzang arrived at the country of Gaochang (the present Turpan area). The king of Gaochang personally received him and persuaded him to stay there. Xuanzang kindly refused his goodwill and resolutely went ahead. The king offered him a great amount of gold and silver as well as 30 horses and servants to help him during his journey. Xuanzang continued toward Tianshan Mountain. When they crossed over the snow-covered mountains, a great number of horses and helpers died of cold weather. After nearly two years of difficult and dangerous journey, Xuanzang arrived at Nalanda Temple in India.

At that time, Nalanda Temple was India's highest institute of learning and Buddhist Holy Land. It had 10,000 monks and visiting Buddhist scholars. They studied Mahayana classics, medicine, logic, important documents and techniques. There were 10 senior monks, who were able to explain 50 titles of Scripture texts. The leader of the Temple was Master Jiexian, respected as Great Master.

Xuanzang was very popular in this Temple and enjoyed the highest respect. He even entitled to ride an elephant as means of transportation, a special honour reserved for high rank monk. He formally had been accepted Jiexian as his official student, studied there for 5 years, and finally was promoted as deputy master monk. In AD 643, Xuanzang was invited to preach Buddhist Scripture in the city of Kanyakubja. Present at the event were kings from 18 countries and more than 3,000 monks. Xuanzang achieved a high degree of honor and was acknowledged as a first-class scholar in India.

Xuanzang studied various schools of Buddhism and established deep friendship with Indian monks. The king of India persuaded Xuanzang

A portrait of Monk Xuanzhuang.　　　　*A mural painting in the 3rd cave of Shanxi Yuelin.*

to stay in India and promised to build 100 temples for him. However, Xuanzang yearned for his motherland and hoped to return home as soon as possible. The king cannot but reluctantly bid farewell to the great scholar from the east.

In the spring of AD 645, at the age of 44, Xuanzang returned to Chang'an. He brought with him the Buddhism classics, collected in India and sent them to Hongfu Temple of Chang'an. From downtown Zhuque Street to the Hongfu Temple, Xuangzang received hero's welcome

曆三年戊申□四百四年又至今大唐庚午即四百九十六

通六年正□十五日記

大像高一百廿尺開皇時中僧善喜造講堂從初　至大

大像高一百卅尺又開元年中僧處諺與鄉人馬思忠等造南

可有五百餘合龕又至延載二年禪師靈隱共居士陰　等造北

二僧晉司空索靖題壁号仙巖寺自茲以后鐫　不絕

多諸神異復於傳師合龕側又造一龕伽從監之　之摩於

之狀遂架空焉嚴大造合龕像次有法良禪師東來

門樂傳伏錫西遊至此巡礼其山見金光如千仏

右在州東南廿五里三危山上秦建元之世有沙

莫高窟記

The Journal of Mogaoku, *in the 156th cave of Dunhuang, compiled in AD 865.*

by the people lined dozens of miles. Xuanzang had audience with Tang Emperor Taizong and the Emperor granted him to devote his life to the translating of Buddhist Scripture in the Hongfu Temple.

In AD 648, crown prince Li Zhi ordered to build the luxurious Ci'en

Temple in commemoration of the death of his mother. Xuanzang was ordered to move to the new temple. In AD 652, Xuanzang personally took part in the transportation of bricks and stone to build a tall Buddha Tower. That is the present Dayan Tower in Xi'an. Although Dayan Tower had undergone several major renovations, the main structure remained the same and it has, become a valuable monument. In AD 664, Xuanzang died in Yuhua Temple of Chang'an at the age of 63.

Xuanzang was well versed both in Chinese and Sanskrit. His translation was accurate and fluent. The translation workshop under his leadership educated and trained many translation elites, elevating Chinese translation level to a new high. He also introduced Indian logic to China, promoting the development of logic in China.

The spirit of Xuanzang is still highly respected all over the world today. Indian people regard him as a sage. Indian museum displays his images of searching for Scripture. His *Da-Tang Xi-Yu Ji* (Tang Dynasty Travels in the Western Regions) recorded what he had seen and heard in more than 130 state-cities. The book wrote about their geographies, histories, climates, products, natural environment and social customs. It is not only an exquisite literary work, but also a famous historic and geographic work. It has been translated into English, French, Japanese and many other foreign languages. Many countries had institutes and societies devoted solely to the studies on Xuanzang. For example, in 1961 Japanese academic community organized the Society of Xuanzang.

Sogdians, the Rich Merchant and Artist on the Silk Road

According to the archeological evidence, the Sogdians were originated from Scythians on the Asian continent. Around 10th century BC they were scattered along the middle reaches of the Amu Darya River. Sogdians believed in Zoroastrianism. Like all the Islamic nations in Iranian Plateau, the Sogdians worshiped Ahura Mazda, the God of the Universe. They regarded the structure of the Universe as the struggle between the light and the black. Ancient Chinese called the religion of Sogdians as "Xianjiao."

In 2nd century BC the Sogdians established their country which was called Kangju. Before that, the Sogdians had long built up ancient cities of Aflaciab and Malakanda in the present Samarkand. They utilized the trade route between Asia and Europe to establish commercial links with India and cities on the northern banks of the Black Sea. The peoples of Sogdiana and Khorezm jointly created Kangju culture – an important milestone of Central Asian culture in the 4th centuries BC.

Around AD 550, Turks controlled the whole Central Asia. Although the Sogdians were subordinate to Turks, they always mastered their traditional occupation, commerce and trade. Sogdians enjoyed exceptional advantages in trade with northern Chinese. According to the religious documents of Dunhuang, Sogdians were possibly the followers of Buddhism and Manicheism.

Sogdians moved from the rich valleys of Zelavshan River to Yumen Pass, and finally settled in Lanzhou. Some of them also migrated to China's Central Plains, in pursuing their customers for their trade. It is possible that they built up trade firms and appointed agent between Kangju and northern China where they even had permanent settlements. They employed some occupational caravans. They traveled frequently through Koucha-niya, Ichtikhan, Samarkand, and Osrouchana.

In the period of AD 550-670, Sogdians gained considerable achievements in the fields of agriculture, industry, commerce, arts and culture. In agriculture, they transplanted two kinds of Samarkand cherries in royal gardens; they learned the Kyaris method (an irrigation system of wells connected by underground channels) from the people of Tarim Basin. Around AD 640, they introduced the technique of brewing wine to Chinese hinterland. Chinese people for the first time enjoyed the delicious wine. The mysterious fruit – "gold peach" was also spread from Kangju area to China's Central Plains.

Sogdian craftsmen were good at arts. Their wood engraving skill spread all over Central Asia. Their wool fabrics and rugs were well known to the world. Their cotton textiles were famous for their high quality. Their metallic armors were strong. They were possibly the inventors of this craftwork. However, according to Chinese historic records, Chinese once taught other people how to make metallic armors. Anyway, the Samarkand armors had enjoyed a great reputation until the end of Medieval Ages.

At that time, Sogdians had already been able to manufacture high-grade colored glaze. In 5th century, they exported this technique to Chinese. Sogdians sold colored glaze products to its adjacent areas. Before long, Chinese lost interests in the manufacturing of colored glazes,

Filaments of ancient wooden knit ware found in Lop Nor, showing a Roman Hermes portrait.

because they themselves invented a new technique of porcelain making. Since the beginning of 7th century, China began to manufacture world-renowned porcelains.

Sogdians sold spices, fabrics, horses, jewelries and colored glaze wares. They bought back batches of raw silks from Chinese and sold them to Persians, Byzantines, Indians and nomadic tribes in the prairies. Sogdians were natural traders, making trade deals with these nationalities and tribes on the oasis near the Aral Sea and purchased from them the hides, leather costumes and muskiness.

At the same time, the sea trade between the East and the West via sea route enjoyed a similar prosperity. This sea route run through Ceylon, which was free from various interventions and able to develop economy stably and freely. Ceylon provides a haven for monks persecuted and ousted from Indo-China Peninsular. These monks in turn made contributions for the spread of Buddhism.

The Rising of Arabs

The Arabian Empire was rising almost at the same time as Chinese Tang Dynasty. It is a multi-national Islamic country, stretching across 3 continents of Asia, Africa and Europe.

There were many coincidences in the ups and downs of the Arabian Empire and the Tang Dynasty. Around AD 613, Mohammed began to preach and publicize Islamism. Afterwards, he achieved a series of victories in his military actions. The forces were strengthened continually. In AD 630, his army occupied Mecca and established a dominating position for Islamism in the Arabian Peninsula. In decades of jihad, the Arabian empire defeated Byzantium, successively occupied Palestine, Iraq, Syria, Mesopotamia and Egypt, and conquered the whole territory of Persia.

At the same time, Li Yuan, the founder of Tang Dynasty, began to train cavalry and assembled strong forces in Shanxi. In AD 618, he established the Great Tang Dynasty. After a series of wars, he unified China around AD 625. In the following years between AD 626 and 649, Tang Dynasty became increasingly powerful and strong, defeated the Turks and resumed the territories in the Western Regions. In AD 650-755, under the rules of Tang Gaozong, Wu Zetian and Tang Emperor X'uanzong, Tang Dynasty reached the heyday of the empire and entered a most flourishing and prospering period in China's empirical history.

A sculpture of Sphinx, collected by Musol Museum, Iraqi.

Although Tang Dynasty inevitably collided with the Arabian Empire in its expansion in Central Asia, the two empires coexisted friendly for most of the time. Since 8th century, the trade and commercial relations between Arab and China became more and more frequent. They depended both on the land road in the north and west and on the sea route in the south. At that time, many merchants come to China from the Arabian-controlled areas most of them being Persians. They brought with them expensive jewelries and medicines to Gansu, Shaanxi and even Sichuan.

Many terracotta warriors made in the style of the tri-colored porcelains of Tang Dynasty were popular to be buried with Arabian rich and powerful. These terracotta warriors looked like Arabians with tall noses, wearing steeple-crown hats, holding Xiyu musical instruments in the arm or leading along camels or horses. Within the territory of the Arabian Empire, there were many cities, including Baghdad in particular, marketing Chinese silk, tea, bullion wares and porcelains.

The celadon and colored trays, excavated in Teheran and other Arabian cities, are the testimony of bustling scene of the Arabian and Persian businessmen on the Silk Road. In the tombs of Tang Dynasty near Xi'an, silver coins of Sasanian Dynasty and gold coins of Arabian empire were discovered. In Xinjiang, Arabian silver coins and Persian gold bars was unearthed which dated 17th century. These were the currencies brought to China by Persian and Arabian businessmen.

Arabian and Persian traders also traveled to China by sea. They sailed from Persian Gulf via the Strait of Malacca northward to Jiaozhou and Guangzhou. Chinese called these foreign trade ships "marketing boats."

In the period of Tang Dynasty, lots of Arabians and Persians settled in China as merchants. Most of them lived in Guansgzhou and Chang'an. Some of Persian merchants also settled in Yangzhou, Hongzhou and Zhangye. Records indicated that some of Arabians even took part in official Chinese examination to be selected as mandarins. For example Li Yansheng, a Persian, was recommended to take part in the highest level of imperial examinations, interviewed by the Emperor in person and became a senior scholar. This fully demonstrated liberal Tang Dynasty provided many opportunities for all.

Islamism had great impacts on the eastern and western section of Silk Road. Along the Silk Road in the desert were many Muslim-styled buildings which were integrated into the local architecture and became important landmarks.

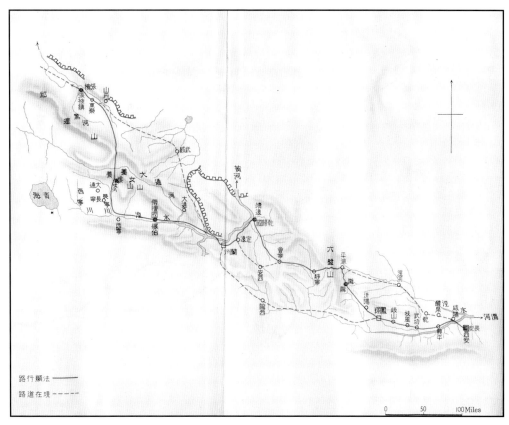

A sketch map showing the route Monk Faxian took after he left Chang'an (1).

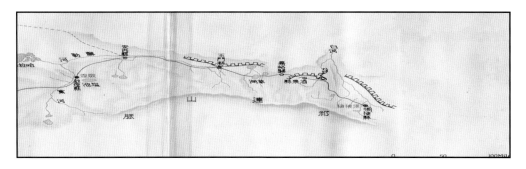

A sketch map showing the route Monk Faxian took after he left Chang'an (2).

97

Buddha in 285th cave at Dunhuang during western Wei period (AD 535 to 556).

From Wudai (Five Dynasty) period to Song Dynasty, under the local authority, Dunhuang enjoyed a long period of prosperity and the local economy developed rapidly. The art and culture continued the tradition of Tang Dynasty. A mural paiting in the 61st cave at Dunhuang, illustrating the story of Shakya Muni.

Kings listening to preaching at 61st Dunhuang cave.

99

A Tang period tri-coloured pottery of camel merchant.

A Tang period pottery figure.

Three musicians playing their instrument on the mural painting in 231st Dunhuang cave. Reading from the face features, they are of non Chinese origin.

An Eastern Han period porcelain figure

An ancient Indian sculpture in the 13th century

A globe drawing, in 1240.

A world map, in 1519, collected by French National Library.

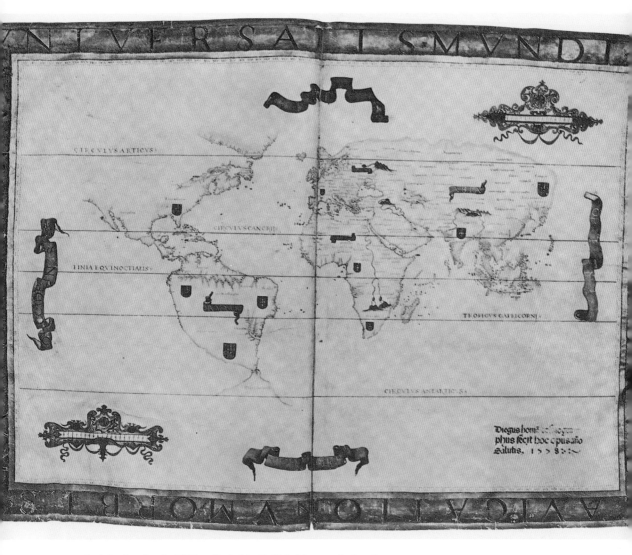

A globe drawing in 1558, collected by British Museum in London.

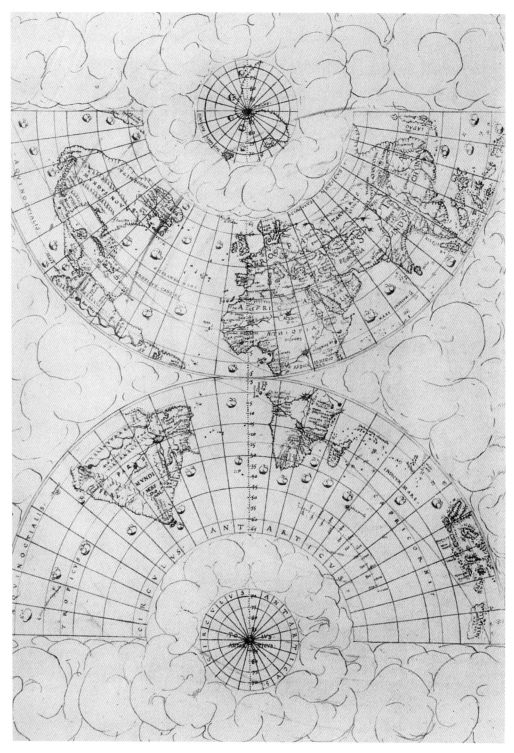

A world map in 1561, collected by French National Library.

Merchant ship during 16th Centure between China by India to Europe

A Yuan dynasty period blue and white porcelain vase

A map of Taranto Italy, a port city which has a long history with the East. During the 1986 invasion by British and French allied army to Beijing, the "Yong Le Encyclopedia" was first brought back to Taranto.

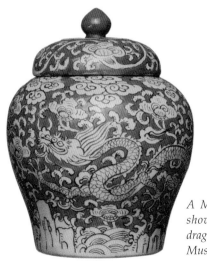

A Ming period pottery showing red foundation dragon pattern, collected by Musee Guimet, France.

A Ming period blue and white porcelain vase, collected in Lisbon.

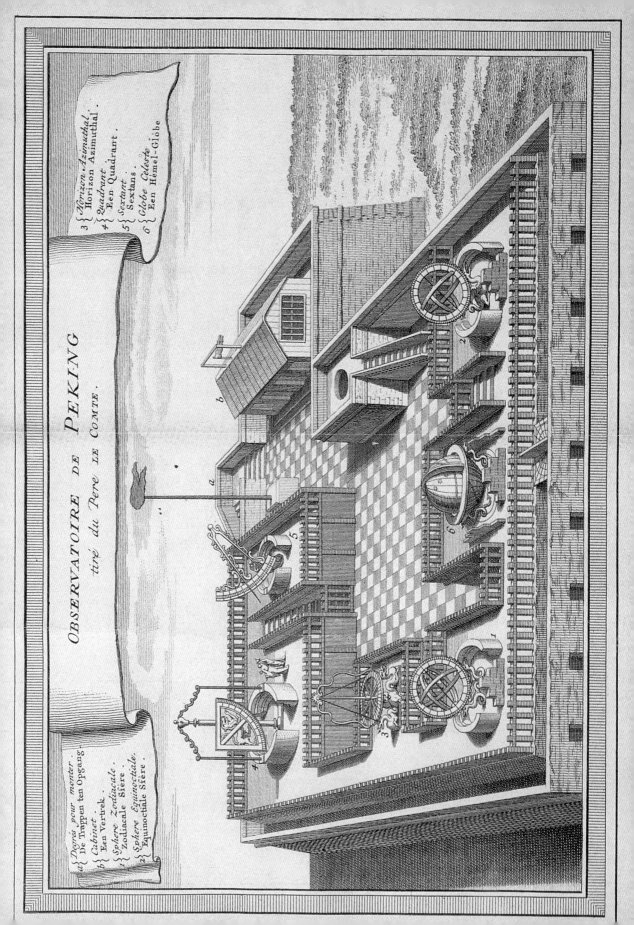

OBSERVATOIRE DE PEKING
tiré du Pere LE COMTE.

a {Degrés pour monter.
   De Trappen ten Opgang.
b {Cabinet.
   Een Vertrek.
1 {Sphere Zodiacale.
   Zodiacale Sfere.
2 {Sphere Equinoctiale.
   Equinoctiale Sfere.

3 {Horizon Azimuthal.
   Horizon Azimuthal.
4 {Quadrant.
   Een Quadrant.
5 {Sextant.
   Sextans.
6 {Globe Celeste.
   Een Hemel-Globe.

The Influence of Roman Arts on the Oriental Cultures

In the first AD centuries, Egypt and India established close com mercial relations. As a consequence of the trade and commerce, Egyptian arts had considerable impacts on the Buddhist Early Greek-styled. Today Early Greek-style arts were extraordinarily preserved in many ancient Buddhist sites and especially on their mural paintings.

In 1906-1907, Stein in eastern Lop Nor area of Tarim Basin exca-vated several large mural paintings, which were kept intact because of the dry weather in the desert. In 14th-15th centuries, In 1946-1947, So-viet archeological expedition team headed by Dolsdov, also made an thorough investigation of the Toprak-kala Frescos near Khorezm.

Stein made systematic research and investigation on the ancient rel-ics he discovered, in which a great amount of items were associated with Chinese Han Dynasty and Indian civilization. He for the first time discovered frescos of Early Greek-style times in an ancient Buddhist temple. He said, when he saw ancient artworks as old as cherubim arts, he simply couldn't believe his eyes. He wrote afterwards, "The patterns and colors of these frescos are classicality in the real sense. They are older than anything I have seen before." The persons in the pictures

Two Cherubim painting in Lop Nor, discovered by Stein.

had big, shining eyes; small, chubby lips; and eagle noses. The whole scenes illustrated Fayum and Roman styles. The paintings indicated that the artists from the Mediterranean Sea had a direct influence in the Buddhist paintings.

Stein told us, "These were young men and wore Frigian-styled hats. Although their faces look like women, the outline of their faces appears like the God of Sun all the Roman Empire worshiped. The male heads had varied features and some of them styled after Romans." Stein also discovered the images of some young girl whose faces resembled the images of Greek or Cherks.

One fresco told a story in the life of Buddha. Columns of solider and horses on the painting looked like the victory parade in Roman Empire. The second fresco seems to be drawn by the same artist. Stein assumed, when drawing the two religious frescos, the artist had to follow the practice of European arts while respecting the rules of traditional Buddhist arts. While drawing secular pictures, he freely used Oriental skills. The artist was possibly born in northern India or central Asia, brought up in an environment of Buddhism and educated by Western artist masters. That was the reason why he was welll aware of the practice of Buddhist arts and at the same time well versed in the Western arts.

Miran was the furthermost eastern center where the relics of "Romanized" arts were discovered. Stein considered that these frescos were such important historical documents and they had to be moved to a safe and reliable place for their safe keeping. At first, he tried to take pictures of them. However by exposure to the flush, the original color would be damaged. Moreover, these frescos were painted on the walls of a narrow corridor, so that there was no room to take pictures. Therefore, he decided to move these frescos elsewhere. He first peeled the frescos off the walls, and then flatly put them in woolen boxes. This preparation lasted 3 years and eventually these frescos were safely moved back to the British Museum.

More than 40 years later, a Soviet expedition headed by Dorsdov, investigated the Central Asian part of the Soviet Union and systematically surveyed the Great Castle of Topra-kala. The Castle is situated on the right side of the Amu Darya River and 150-160 kilometers to the coast of the Aral Sea. Its three 25-meter-high towers overlooked the whole city. This great castle was once the capital of a kingdom.

The team led by Dorsdov excavated a great deal of fresco pavilions in the Castle. These frescos were painted on clay walls, in traditional Early Greek-style art. Others were in art styles of Roman times. The painted figures had the features of people in Syria, Egypt and the Black Sea regions. Dorsdov wrote, "On the walls of a pavilion exist two different traditions, one being integrated with the other." Both Early Greek-style arts and the "Western arts in Roman times" were evident in the paintings.

At the other end of this trade route is Qielan area, where Chinese woolen and silk textiles were excavated in some graves. These textiles were possibly used as cerecloths. As far as artistic style and technique were concerned, these textiles were similar to the silk relics Stein discovered in Lolan. This indicated that the two textile nations were likely to have developed technical exchanges. In Qielan area were also excavated some single-colored Damascus-styled brocade decorative textiles. They were very thick. Their patterns on both sides were completely the same. On the one hand, they had the patterns of Damascus-styled brocade decorative textiles; on the other, they were quite like the taffeta raw silk, which could be used as cloth linings. The integration of these two techniques represents a well-developed spinning and weaving skills. It is generally acknowledged that Chinese people initiated and developed these skills.

At that time, Lop Nor area was considered a converging point for industrial and artistic exchanges. From the above-mentioned ancient Miran frescos, it can be seen that the impact Rome had on the region.

In Miran, lots of Han Dynasty copper coins were discovered, indicating the presence of Han merchants.

In the excavations in Lop Nor area, Stein discovered one Chinese styled female slipper in the armrest of a Early Greek-styled easy chair. The slipper was milk-white woolen knitwear with embroidered geometrical patterns. It reminds of the Coptic or Byzantine styles. This simple Chinese slipper in Roman art pattern once more illustrated that the influences of the Roman Empire and Chinese tradition on the art in the countries east of the Mediterranean Sea.

Early Greek-style paintings were a little later than the Miran frescos. Most of them appeared in Kuqa. The Kezir Thousand-Buddha Caves near Kuqa was a treasure house of Early Greek-style arts. In the cave of painters, there was a self-portrait of a painter. The painter wore cavalier-styled frock with hairs drooping down over his shoulders, holding Chinese brush pen in his right hand and palette in his left hand. The signature appeared on the painting was Mitradatta. This was a typical Greek name. The Greek name and Byzantine costume indicated the painter should be a Byzantine.

The Xiyu frescos discovered near Turpan belonged to 7th to 10th centuries. Reading from these frescos it was evident that Roman artistic style still had an active influence until 8th century. In the early 20th century, Grenweder and Kohk of Germany took these frescos off from their cave walls and moved them to the National Museum in Berlin. In the process, many original paintings were seriously damaged. On the frescos of Idikut-Sahri, there were women wearing Greek-styled clothes and hats. Buddha and Bodhisattva were in their typical sit posture appeared on some mural paintings. The style of angels and painting technique on the Sangim frescos were the same to that on the frescos of Kuqa and Bamian, indicating the travel route of the art style from Bamian through Kuqa to Idikut-Sahri.

The Culture Diversity of the Silk Road

Turpan

In Chinese history Turpan was an important and unique city on the Silk Road for the culture exchange and integration. It witnessed the complicated process of administering the Western Regions by Han and Tang dynasties. The Turpan Basin connects Hexi Corridor in the east to Tarim Basin in the west. Therefore, it was a strategically important place. Han Dynasty fought with the Hun for the control of this strategic city. After many fierce battles, the increasingly powerful Western Han Kingdom eventually succeeded in controlling the Silk Road and occupied this city of strategic importance. And the Hun was never to be able to recover from the setback.

After Han Dynasty, owing to the political upheavals, The kingdom of Gaochang started to rule the area. Under the support of Rouran, a nomadic tribe in the north, Gaochang occupied the whole Turpan Basin. In the early 6th century, Gaochang became a subordinate to Turke. In 7th century, after Tang Dynasty defeated Turkes, Gaochang collapsed and the area became Xizhou under the jurisdiction of Tang Dynasty.

In AD 327, Zhang Jun of Pre-Liang occupied Turpan and established the County of Gaochang. The city of Gaochang was chosen as its capital city. For 140 years, the ancient city of Gaochang developed rapidly and became a famous prosperous metropolis on the Silk Road.

Since Western Han Dynasty exercised jurisdiction over the Western Regions, a large number of Han people migrated to Gaochang and Chinese culture became broadly accepted in the region. The fact that mausoleums of the rich and powerful families used extensively the Chinese decorations was reminiscent to the popularity of Chinese culture in the region. The mural-paintings on the tomb chambers vividly described the social life in Jin, Sui and Tang dynasties. The topics of these frescos included most aspects of life for example, touring on horseback, singing and dancing of nobles as well as farming and laboring of common people and soldiers. Many items buried with the dead and excavated in modern times were silk costumes, musical instruments, fruit and vegetables, and pens, paper and ink, all of which were real items used during that period. The most famous excavation is the "Turpan documents," a collection of recorded trade exchanges and the lists of commodities available.

When he went westward for Buddhist Scripture, Xuanzang stayed in Gaochang and preached the Buddhism for one month. He was well received by the king of Gaochang. Gaochang was unique among the countries of the Western Regions and it was famous for its magnificent temples and Buddhist ceremonies.

Yutian: the west Buddhism Center in Tang Dynasty

Yutian (the present Hotan in Xinjiang) was a famous city on the Silk Road. It was widely known to the outside world for its beautiful jades. Although it was situated at the southern-western edge of the Taklamakan Desert the Yutian River (the present Hotan River) and other rivers flowed through the area, irrigating fertile land It was an oasis with abundant natural plantations. It was the richest place in the Western Regions.

From ancient times, Yutian had been producing beautiful jades, which were transported eastwards. The jade articles, excavated from the ruins of Shang Dynasty in Anyang, were mostly made of Yutian jades.

There were a great variety of Yutian jades. Some crystal white, some emerald green, some black and some yellow. The trading of jades was profitable and therefore many merchants both local and from far away engaged in the trade. Yutian jades traveled as far as Parthia and the rest of the Western Regions.

The beautiful jades brought both fame and prosperity to Yutian. After the opening of the Silk Road and the Western Regions established closer relations with China, Yutian, stood on the southern section of the Silk Road, became an even more important trade city. With the increased trade and cultural exchanges between the West and East, Yutian learnt sericulture and silk reeling and weaving technique and became a silk manufacture base in the Western Regions.

Because of its strategic position, a rich variety of natural products and multi-cultural influence, Yutian became an early receiver of Buddhism. When Faxian arrived at Yutian on his travel westward for Scripture, Yutian was a important centre for Buddhist ceremonies. There were luxurious grandiose temples with tens of thousands monks. When he went to Tenjiku via Yutian, Xuanzang witnessed a solemn ceremony for the image of Buddha. This was a grand annual festival in Yutian. Xuanzang made a detailed record of what he had seen. Owing to the prevailing Buddhist ceremonies, the country of Yutian served as a center of Buddhism in the Western Regions.

Since the beginning of the 20th century, many excavation efforts were made to unearth the sites of Buddhist temples in the territory of Hotan and the adjacent areas. When he was in Hotan, Stein participated in several excavation work and unearthed lots of Early Greek-style images of Buddha. It was clear that Yutian received heavy influences both from India and Persia, and at the same time the influence of the imported cultures integrated well with the Han culture of China's hinterland. In addition, Arabian, West-Asian, Mongolian, Tibetan and Western Christian cultures were also reflected in Yutian's historic relics.

In AD 632, the king of Yutian dispatched envoy to offer jade belt to Tang emperor Taizong. Soon after he sent his son to serve in Tang empirical court. When Tang army conquered Kizil the king of Yutian immediately rewarded the army generously. He followed the general of the victorious Tang army to Chang'an to have had an audience with the emperor. Tang Emperor Gaozong bestowed him a dwelling house many silk cloths and gold belts. He stayed in the capital for several months. His image was carved in a tombstone which was erected at the mausoleum of Tang emperor Taizong.

Cave Arts with Good Combination of Chinese and Foreign Influences

According to ancient documents, at the time of the 3rd to 4th century, there were more and more Kizil Buddhist monks coming to Chinese hinterland to translate the Buddhist Scripture. In the middle of the 4th century, there were more than 10,000 Buddhist monks in Kizil alone. It was under this historical background that Kezir caves were created and gradually expanded. At first, Hinayana prevailed in Kizil. Later, senior monk Kumarajiva energetically advocated Mahayana. The king of Kizil gave him courteous reception on his arrival. The wall paintings in Kezir stone caves vividly depicted the prevailing of Hinayana and that followed by Mahayana. In the 8th century, because of the increase of Buddhist temples, the cave arts began to decline. In 14th century, Mongols ruled Kuqa area, and forcibly advocated the teaching of Islam During the process Kezir cave arts were severely damaged. Although no

Mural paintings in the 7th Cave of Kezir Thousand-Buddha caves.

carved images of Buddha remained lots of the preserved frescos recorded and displayed the bygone prosperity. It was clear that the Kezir stone caves occupied an important position in the Central Asian and in the history of Buddhist stone caves. Today the remaining Kezir frescos and the excavated relics are invaluable treasures for the study of Buddhism.

The gorgeous cave arts in Kizil were closely related to the frequent cultural exchanges between the East and the West. It is worthy to mention that in Kizil frescos there were delicately painted naked figures, especially female bodies. In many Buddhist preaching, there were often graceful naked girls sitting or lying before the Buddha. All the singing and dancing Bodhisattvas were also naked on the cave paintings. The figures of dancing girls had their wonderful bodies, fleshy breasts and erogenous hips in an exaggerating way. In some of the cave frescos, there were even pictures of sexual intercourse. These brave and broad-minded depictions revealed the deep influence of Greek human body, Indian Buddhist and Early Greek-style arts. The original aesthetic standards of Kizil artists skillfully combined secular and religious tastes. These exquisite drawing and innovative naked images are masterpieces in the history of cave arts.

Buddhist cave arts in Gaochang site are the valuable historic and cultural heritages of the Western Regions. In Gaochang, the local Buddhism was deeply influenced by the religious faith of the Han Nationality and the local customs. The art integrated with the arts of Early Greek-style and Indian Buddhism, so that Gaochang arts were different from those of Kizil. These social characteristics and special art style were vividly reflected in Gaochang cave frescos.

Between the Singing Sand Mountain and Sanwei Mountain, 25 kilometers to the south-east of Dunhuang city, there stood the famous Mogao Caves. The carving of the caves began in AD 366. The following generations of kingdoms continued the undertaking. Today there are 492 caves with more than 2,400 colored statues and 45000 square meters of mural paintings in Mogao, five wooden buildings of Tang Dynasty and Song Dynasty styles. The depth of caves amounts to 1,600 meters. If all the cave paintings were lined side by side, it will be a gallery of 25 km. It is truly a wonder in the world history of arts. Mogao Caves also kept more than 60,000 volumes of hand-copied Buddhist texts, official documents and silk paintings. Today they are one of the most important historic and cultural treasures in the world.

The mural paintings on the Mogao Caves are themselves art monument. They vividly depict the wonderful Buddhist paradise and visualize the aspects of ancient art, cultural and social lives of China and other regions. The paintings on the Mogao Caves also had very rich local flavors and at the same time absorbed the influences of Buddhist cultures from Central, Southern and Western Asian.

Internal layout and decoration of rock cave at Dunhuang.

The earliest recording of mural painting in the Dunhuang's Thousand Buddha Caves.

The Foreign Religions Practiced in China

Jingjiao (Christian Historian section)

Christianism was introduced to China in AD 3rd-4th centuries. At the end of 3rd century, Anobis, a Roman writer, recorded in his book Adversus Gentes II, 12 the process how Christian teaching came to China and India. In the 5th century, Nestorian Christians entered the hinterland of China which provided another period for Christianity to expand rapidly in China. Christianity was called "Jingjiao" in Tang Dynasty.

Niestuorius, a Syrian, was the founder of the Nestorian Christians, and assumed the post of archbishop in Constantinople between A.D 428 to 431. He advocated a new theory that Jesus was both a human and a God. His theory was in contradiction with Egyptian archbishop, who advocated that Jesus was only the God. As a result, Niestuorius was dismissed from his post. In AD 435, he was denounced as a heresy and ousted from Egypt. Niestuorius and his followers had no choice but to go into exile and establish a new church in Persia. He translated Greek scientific and philosophic books, and preached the followers in western and central Asia.

In central Asia, parishes of Helat and Samarkand were established in AD 411-415 and 503-520 respectively. These parishes were collectively responsible for the preaching in China. The establishment of Parish for China was actually delayed until AD 635.

At the turn of 5th and 6th centuries, Jingjiao was officially allowed to preach in Luoyang. Lots of Christian missionaries came to China from foreign countries, including Persia during this period. Tang emperor Taizong adopted an attitude of toleration towards various schools of religions. In March 1625, a Nestorian Temple Tablet dated AD 781 was excavated in Xi'an. This was the first literature records on the introduction of Christianity to China, kept intact to date. Alopen, mentioned in the inscription was either the name of a person or the position of a person who came to China to preach Christianity.

Tang Taizong received Alopen with courtesy and warmth. He was a very far sighted emperor with great talent and broad vision, and allowed different schools of religions to coexist and prosper together. He also took resolute measures to contain the opposition and objection to the new found religions of Confucians.

During the period of Tans Suzong (AD 756-762), the followers of Jingjiao were allowed to live in the royal palace all the times. According to historic records, the construction of 5 Jingjiao churches was attributed to the efforts of Tang Suzong. During the period of Tang Daizong (AD 763-779) when birthday he celebrated his birthday, he would certainly go to in the Jingjiao church to pray and entertained the Jingjiao followers in the Palace. Jingjiao was allowed to preach until AD 845, when the emperor of Tang Dynasty announced a total ban on all religious activities. This ban forced the exile of more than 2,000 followers of Jingjiao and Xianjiao. Since then, both religions gradually disappeared in China.

A Catholic portrait made in Quanzhou, the starting point of sea Silk Road between 1313 and 1362.

A cross erected in Daqin temple in Xi'an in AD 781 during a time when Chinese temple tablets were popular with the Oriental Orthodoxy.

Xianjiao

In the 6th century BC Zoroaster, a Persian, created Xianjiao also known as Zoroastrianism, and it worships fire. In AD 236, Sasanian Dynasty in Persia adopted Zoroastrianism as a State Religion. Sasanian Dynasty combined the state with the church and both were under the rule of its king. For the king of Sasanian Persia, to worship Xianjiao was a mean to incite national sentiment against ancient Greek influence. However, from a more general view, the rulers of Sasanian Dynasty normally adopted a liberal attitude toward other races than their own. They welcomed the Jews and the followers of Nestorian Christians.

The history of Tang Dynasty recorded the spread of Xianjiao in China. However, there was no indication of where the preachers came from. Judging from the cultural relics, excavated so far, most of the tribes in the region believed in Xianjiao.

There was little common ground between Xianjiao and traditional Chinese concepts. The reason why the emperor of Tang Dynasty tolerated the spreading of Xianjiao in China was mainly based on political consideration, because Persia was an ally and trade partner for Tang Dynasty. Xianjiao had not received the same amount of appreciation from the Chinese emperor as the Jingjiao did. Some ideas and practices of Xianjiao were contradictory to Chinese thinking. For example, Xianjiao held that good and evil were in irreconcilable contradiction. The Xianjiao followers used to put dead body on the top of a tower or a mountain for wild animals or raptors to eat up. This funeral practices were totally unacceptable for Chinese, who attached importance to the integrality of the dead body. It seems that they regarded Xianjiao as a foreign religion and an uncivilized faith of an alien race. That was why it never had an important impact on the thought of Chinese. It disappeared from China in AD 845 when the government imposed a ban on all the alien faiths. However, today we can still find the trace of Xianjiao patterns on the silk fabrics from Persian.

Manicheism

Manicheism was created by Mani, a Persian (216-277) in 3rd century. Mani was born in the city of Xuli. He widely studied the teachings of Xianjiao, Christianity and Buddhism, and created Manicheism with the purpose to promote the fight of light against darkness. Mani had been to northern India and western China. He was exiled by the king of Persia. In AD 277 was sentenced to death. and Manicheism was banned. Its followers escaped to Central Asia and India. From 4th to 6th centuries, Manicheism was very popular in northern Africa and the coastal cities of the Mediterranean Sea.

In AD694, Furstadan, also a Persian came to the Kingdom of Tang with the holy book of Erzongjing written by Mani, which was one of the basic classics of Manicheism. The other holy classic Manicheism book was Sanjijing. The remnants of the two classics found in the caves of Dunhuang were kept in the National Library in Beijing, under the title of The Remnants of Persian Church Classics. It was difficult to understand why Manicheism had been well received in China as the basic concept of Manicheism like Xianjiao was in contradiction to the traditional Chinese believes. Lots of important relics related to Manicheism were discovered in Dunhuang.

In early 20th century, many mural paintings of Manicheism were discovered in Central Asia while Xianjiao was mainly preached orally and there were very few books of Xianjiao teaching remained today. Sogdians were at its peak of cultural development and therefore Manicheism was deep rooted in Kangju. When Persia exiled the followers of Manicheism and sentenced its founder Mani to death in the 3rd century, Most Manicheism believers went to Kangju as refuges. In the following centuries, Manicheism made a significant progress and found many believers among Turks. Ancient Uighurs even adpoted Manicheism as its national religion. By and large this determined the attitude of Chinese government to the Manicheism. When Chinese were friendly with Uighurs, they were tolerant to Manicheism. When China was hostile to the Uighurs, the religion would be restricted.

Manicheism was mainly dependent on the influences of Uighurs to gain popularity. In November AD 762, Uighurs khan helped Tang Dynasty defeat the rebel general Shi Chaoyi and occupied Luoyang and stayed in the capital until March AD 763. During his stay in Luoyang, the khan converted from Buddhism to Manicheism. He brought back four Manicheism priests with him when he returned to his country. Under the support of the khan, most Uighurs believed in Manicheism.

Because of the special relations between Tang Dynasty and Uighurs, many Uighurs migrated to Chang'an. In June AD 769, Tang Dynasty officially permitted Uighur followers of Manicheism, to establish temples and their priests were allowed to preach. 3 years later, in AD 771, they built up more temples in Provinces. Followers normally wore white costumes and white hats. In January AD 807, under the advices of Uighurs envoys, three temples were built in Taiyuan. By then Manicheism temples existed both in the north and the south of China. Turpan Basin in Xinjiang was also a center for Manicheism.

Uighurs respected Manicheism priests and considered they were their brothers and even their governors. Whenever Uighur envoys went to the capital of Tang Dynasty, Manicheism priests always accompanied them, serving as policy advisers. There were more and more Manicheism priests in Chang'an.

Islamism

Mohammed, the founder of Islamism once told his believers that "We must seek knowledge even if it is far away in China." He possibly gained his knowledge about China from Jingjiao followers in the Red Sea and Persian Xianjiao followers in the Arabian Peninsula. Soon after the establishment of Islamism, the believers began to preach in China.

It is said that during Shui Dynasty, Muslims arrived at Guangzhou by sea. In AD 616, 101 Moslems were persecuted in Mecca. Zafal led the followers to Abyssinia for asylum. From there Zafal together with Sayadler went to Quanzhou by sea and began to preach Islamism.

In AD 618-626, Islamism was already gaining popularity in China's southern-eastern coastal areas. Today on the Lingshan Mountain in

Quanzhou still exists "saint tomb" of two Islamism priests and a stone monument showed that four other followers were buried. In 1965, an Arabian tombstone was discovered in Quanzhou which was dated AD 650. The inscription reads "The grave of Hussein bin Mohammed Salada. Allah blesses him. Died in March of 29th year of Muslim calendar."

The followers of Manicheism, Xianjiao, Jingjiao and Islamism went to Chang'an following the steps of traders and political envoys. They went to and fro along the route of military conquerors and traders. This almost became a fashion. They sowed the seeds of religions in Chian but most of them failed to sprout. During Tang Dynasty when the authority eagerly seeking for Western knowledge, it was not difficult for a foreign church to set a foot in China, but it was not easy to grow. In fact since the Buddhism was introduced to China no other religions were fully accepted in China.

From the Crusades to Marco Polo

The Crusade and the Conquer of Asia-Europe by the Mongols

During the Medieval Ages, European continent was poor and backward. Trade and commerce was very limited. At that time, Slav merchants transported goods only to Kiev. From there Russians shipped them further to the Black Sea to be marketed in Constantinople and other cities.

Russian merchants used fur, honey, wax and even slaves to swap for silk, luxurious costumes, flax, leather, gold ornaments, wine and spices from Byzantium. Obviously, this barter trade was very much against the Russians. The goods from Byzantium were exquisite and expensive while those from Russians and Slavs were primitive and cheap. The affluence of the Orient was truly admired by the knights and landlords of Europe.

The development of trade stimulated the demand of West European landlords and knights for more luxurious goods. They were anxious to expand their territory and to seek for treasures from the Orient. Under the instigation of the churches, landlords and knights organized a

A portrait of Genghis Khan.

crusade. Many farmers, travelers, criminals and adventurers jointed the crusade. Under the banner to seize back Jerusalem, the City of David, from the non-believers, they waged eight aggressive expeditions from AD 1096 to 1272.

Under the resistance of Arabian people, several crusades ended in failure. Although they failed to get a massive amount of wealth, they acquired some unexpected gifts. After the first crusade in 1095, Europeans occupied Beirut and other cities on the eastern bank of the Mediterranean Sea. Therefore, they could intercept the cargo ships from the east and were able to directly make deals with the Eastern traders without the Arabian brokers. The cargoes included silks cotton textiles and potteries from China; genuine pearls from Ceylon; spices and jewelries from India; and condiments from the islands in the South China Sea. These commodities were small in volume and expensive in value. It was profitable to transport them back to Venice and Genoa in Italy. It was at this time that the trade started to prosper on the coasts of the Mediterranean Sea and Europe once again was on its way to prosperity.

In the second crusade expedition in 1164, the king of Sicily occupied Thebes, Kolins and Aden. He took captive the craftsmen of sericulture and silk spinning and weaving and escorted them back to Sicily. A number of local Italian workshops soon were able to manufacture high-quality silk fabrics with various beautiful patterns. At long last, Italy could make its own silk fabrics and no longer had to buy these expensive goods in the east with gold as it did in the times of Caesar.

A Mongol in the 13th century.

Just when Arabia was in its peak of its development and Europe began to its way to prosperity, an unexpected danger from the east befell on them. In the Mongolian plateau, Genghis Khan led a powerful and strong army of cavalries and marched westward in AD 1219. In 1220, Mongolian army attacked and occupied the commercial cities of Samarkand and Bukhara in Central Asia. It continued its march along the valley of the Amu Darya River and Syr Darya River toward Khorezm. After a fierce battle, the Mongols took the capital of Khorezm. Afterwards, Mongolian army turned southward, captured a great number of cities.

In 1222, Mongolian army crossed Taihe Mountain (the present Caucasian Mountain) and marched northward to Kipchak. An Russian allied army entered into a decisive battle with the Mongolian army in Arigy River valley (in present Ukraine) and ended in a total defeat. In

1237, Mongolian army marched further westward, captured Moscow, Rostov, Vlagimir and other cities and conquered a vast expanse of Kipchak and Russian territories.

In 1244, Mongolian army began westward expedition to fight Magyar (Hungary). The cavalries of Asian set feet on East Europe for the first time. The Mongolian army crossed the Vistula River and attacked Cracow. Soon it crossed the Oder River and fought with Teutons. It defeated the Teuton crusade cavalries. Another regiment of the Mongolian army reached the Danube River and captured the city of Pest.

The final attack of the Mongolian army was against Arabia. In 1257, Mongolian army arrived at Persia and attacked Abbasid Dynasty. In the following year it occupied the capital of Arabia, captured and killed the king, and the Mongolian army went rampant and massacred the city for 17 days. This rich and prosperous city was totally destroyed.

The brave Mongols established an unprecedented gigantic empire. Their barbaric conquering destroyed numerous prosperous and bustling cities. Many years elapsed, but the mention of the name of Genghis Khan would still make one's heart flutter with fear. Europe for the first time felt the real existence of the east.

In the past, because Byzantium and Arabia prevented the direct contact between Europe and the east, Europe's knowledge about the east was scarce and patch and many of them were based on legendry and myth. The western expedition of the Mongolian army cuased a great panic among Europeans. In order to ascertain the whereabouts of this "nation on the back of horses," the Roman pontificate dispatched an Italian priest Plan Carpin to Mongolia in AD 1245. The priest of aged at 65 set out from Lyons and reached Kiev via Poland. He met with a Mongolian leader by the Volga River and attended the enthronement ceremony of Guiyou Khan. He returned via the same route and reported back to the pontificate about the military information of the Mongolian army. This was the first official contact between the West and the East.

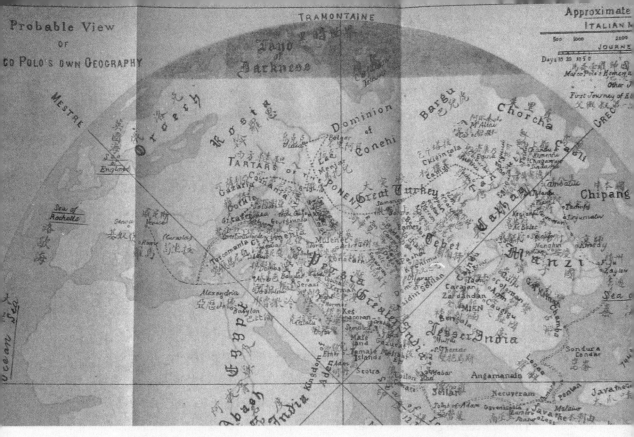

A map of Euroasia by Marco Polo.

The westward expedition of the Mongolian army not only made the Europeans realize the presence of the East, but also brought about another result: The road between the East and the West was open again. Various barriers of Arabia and Khorezm, that stood in the way of commercial exchanged between the Euro-Asian continents, no longer existed with conquering of these countries by the Mongols. European businessmen could travel to the East freely. The Orient was so attractive to adventurous traders and many of them made the journey to the east to see the land of prosperity for themselves. Marco Polo was one of them.

Marco Polo and his adventure to the East

In the 13th century, Italy's Venice was a beautiful and prosperous commercial city on the Mediterranean Sea. There were lots of shrewd traders, sailing the Mediterranean Sea and busing traveling between the Middle East North Africa and Europe.

Because of the separation by Arabian land, the Christians in Europe never entered the Indian Ocean. There is no historic record about Europeans doing business in India and China. Ignorance led Europeans to believe that Jerusalem was the ultimate end of the world and the African coastal lines were too long to cross. After the western expedition of the Mongolian army, Venice merchants Nicolo-polo and Maffeo-polo began to go through the Arabian land to reach China by land.

In 1260, two Polo brothers set off to the coast of the Black Sea. They arrived at Salai, the capital of Kipchak. After they stayed there for one year they continued their journey eastward. They stayed in Bukhara for 3 years and met an envoy from Mongolia. He invited them to visit China. They agreed to go.

In the summer of 1265, they reached Kaiping region (in the present Inner Mongolia). Kublai Khan warmly received the two brothers. After listened to their briefing on Europe, the emperor of the Yuan Dynasty decided to dispatch an envoy to the Vatican. After he was sick on the way, the envoy handed the credential of Kublai Khan to Polo brothers and asked them to bring it to Rome. In 1269, Polo brothers returned to Accra and successfully accomplished their mission. They completed the first trans-Euro-Asian continent travel in the history.

In the November of 1271, Polo brothers once again set off for China but this time they had the reply of the pontificate to Kublai Khan and the 17-year old Marco Polo the son of Nicolo Polo.

They left Venice to start their journey by sea and landed on the eastern coast of the Mediterranean Sea. They went eastward by land along the ancient Silk Road, sometimes on foot, or on horseback, or on camelback. Their first stop was Baghdad. When they arrived, the city had somehow recovered from the invasion of Mongolian army, and restored at least partially its former glory or prosperity. They passed the port Hormuz (the present Abas in Iran) in the Persian Gulf, turned northward and arrived at Bahlaka. They didn't go to Samarkand, but traveled straight eastward, in 12 days crossed over the Pamirs, and entered Kashgar.

They continued their journey eastward along the southern route of the Tarim Basin. They spent a whole month to cross the Lop Nor desert and eventually they arrived at Sazhou (Dunhuang). The whole territory of Xinjiang had become the territory of the Muslims. It was in Sazhou that Marco Polo saw Buddhism temples and but the prosperous scenes of the Tang Dynasty had gone forever. They passed Yumen, Zhangye and Wuwei. They didn't use the traditional route along the Silk Road to Chang'an. They prepared the provision of food and drinking water for 40 days and crossed the desert and arrived at the traveling imperial palace of Chahannaoer. From there they went northeastward for 3 day and reached the capital of the Yuan Dynasty.

When seeing the palace of Kublai Khan, Marco Polo was deeply impressed. He wrote in his travel notes, "The palace is built with marbles and various beautiful and precious stones. Its design is ingenious and sophisticated. All the halls and chambers in the palace were decorated with gold." The court officials told him that the Khan only came here in the summer. His grand palace was actually in the capital of Khan-baliq (the present Beijing).

It was in the summer of 1275 that Marco Polo reached the capital of the Tang Dynasty. Kublai Khan received the young man in the imperial palace, and liked the young man from Europe very much. He even gave him a post in the palace. He stayed in China for 17 years. During his stay, Kublai Khan appointed him as the governor of Yangzhou.

Marco Polo gave a detailed description of the capital of Yuan Dynasty (Beijing): "The grand halls in the palace are majestic and magnificent. The design and architecture are perfect with full of skills

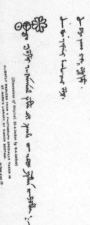

Books of Marco Polo.

and arts." The whole new capital was within a square land surrounded by city walls. The design of the city was defined by straight lines. If you standing at one tower on the city walls, you could see the tower on the other side of the city in the distance.

There were 12 city gates on the city walls, beyond each of them there was a suburb residential area, each covering a distance of 6-7 kilometers. In the suburbs there were hotels and inns for the merchants with camel caravans. More people lived in the suburbs than in the city. You could buy virtually everything in Chang'an. There were no less than 1,000 carriages arrived at the capital each day.

Full of vitality and curiosity, Marco Polo traveled extensively in China. He had traveled a long-distance journey

A Yuan peiod temple tablet in Mongolian and Chinese.

to southern-western regions, visited Xi'an Chengdu, Yunnan, Dali, Yongchang and other cities on Burma border. Afterwards, he toured the provinces on the southeastern coasts, to the commercial cities of Ji'ning, Huai'an, Yangzhou, Hangzhou and Quanzhou, which were the largest trading ports at that time.

Marco Polo witnessed many things he had never seen in the West. In the north, he saw people used black stones as fuel, once ignited, they were just like charcoal but their flame was more vigorous than that of charcoals. It could burn from dusk to dawn. These stones could provide a great amount of energy. Chinese had known for long what coal could do. In Yuan Dynasty, coal had been extensively used in the Empire. Marco Polo was the first Westerner saw the use of coal and he was the first person to introduce coal to Europe.

In the capital of Yuan Dynasty, Marco Polo found people using paper money for business transaction. The paper money was produced by Khan's mint with official seal and had a value of equal gold and silver. In China, paper money was in use since Tang Dynasty. Businessmen no longer need to carry heavy metal of gold and silver as payment for their goods. Paper money was widely used in North Song Dynasty while Europeans still used gold and silver to conduct transactions. Marco Polo introduced paper money to Europe. The use of paper money facilitated the trade in Europe tremendously.

Marco Polo, his father and uncle were appointed to very important positions by Kublai Khan. They accumulated a great amount of wealth. But they missed homeland. In 1292, when his wife died, Il Gagan, the ruler of the Central Asia, asked Kublai Khan to choose a princess as his new wife. Kublai Khan married Princess Kuokuozhen to II Gagan. Marco Polo and his father and uncle recommended themselves to escort the princess. Kublai Khan agreed and asked Marco Polo also to take his letters to the pontiff and the kings of Britain and France. In the summer of 1292, they led an escort of more than 600 and set off from Quanzhou in 14 big ships. After more than 2 years of sailing, they reached the capital of Il Gagan.

After the completion of their mission, Marco Polo, his father and uncle continued their westward journey. They passed Constantinople, entered the Aegean Sea, and sailed along the familiar sea-route in the Mediterranean Sea. In the winter of 1295, they returned to their native city Venice after 25 years of traveling in the East.

But for an accidental event, the experience of Marco Polo might be forgotten with his death. In 1298, Venice was attacked by another commercial city Genoa. Marco Polo took part in the war against Genoa. Unfortunately, Venice was defeated. Marco Polo was captured and put into in prison. In order to spend the long and torturous life behind the bars, Marco Polo told what he saw and heard in China and the far east to his cellmate, Rusticiano, a writer. The writer recorded his story in French. The manuscript was kept in Paris. The book was what known to the world as The Travel Notes of Marco Polo.

At that time, the book didn't attract the attention of the public. Europe was still a place of medieval backwardness. Ignorance made people difficult to believe China was as rich and prosperous as Marco Polo described. No body believed in Marco Polo and thought he made up his story. Marco Polo died silently in his prison cell. Afterwards, no one had ever taken a great trans-Euro-Asian journey both by land and by sea, as Marco Polo did. More than 200 years later, when Columbus read The Travel Notes of Marco Polo, he began to search for China and India by sea. After the great geographical discoveries of Columbus, people realized the contribution Marco Polo made.

Lyons: the Silk Capital
of the Europe

In the 15th and 16th centuries, Europe experienced the religious re forms and the Renaissance. This lead to some important inventions and discoveries. This marked the end of the Mediaeval Ages and the beginning of modern society in Europe. The discovery of the New World brought great prosperity to the Iberian Peninsula. Portuguese colonized Indonesia and extended its influence to the southern border of China. Afterwards, they were replaced by the British and the Dutch. The trade centers transferred to the coasts of the Atlantic.

At the same time, Europeans replaced the superiority of Muslims in the Indian Ocean. However, in the Western World there was no longer a single powerful and unified power as the Roman Empire. Instead Europe was ruled several small countries and they were at wars with each other. They were well matched in strength, competing for sea supremacy at any cost. All these powers had their ups and downs. There were golden ages for the Portuguese and the Dutch. Because of the language barriers and geographic separation there were no clearly understood process how the silk trade was developed within European. However, as for the silk trade and production in France, it was necessary to mention the silk factories in Lyons.

From the 14th century, the French government was aware of the fact that a great amount of gold flew abroad to purchase silk. Many Italians in France, especially in Lyons, sold silk fabrics in major markets. Most of them came from Genoa and Florence. They became millionaires in the trading of silk.

At that time, Lyons had a large-scale international market. In 1450, Lyons was granted to monopolize the silk trade in whole France. Many Italians tried very hard to settle in Lyons. In 1466, Louis XI of France didn't want to see the Italian merchants make fortunes so easily in his country. In order to prevent 40,000,000-50,000,000 ecus (French currency) flowing abroad to import foreign silk fabrics, Louis XI decreed to set up silk factories (royal handicraft workshops) in Lyons. These workshops made profits to replenish the treasury. Afterwards, the factories in Lyons were moved to Tours and a Silk Association was established in Paris. Tours and Paris processed raw materials from afar. Because raw materials were expensive and in short supply in France, this allowed the Italian brocade and woolen cloth continued to enter into French market.

In order to restrict the trade of Italian firms and to promote the development of French industry, France decreed to prohibit the import of textile. Italians, settled in Lyons, faced serious trade threat and they have no choice but tried to manufacture the textile locally.

Two Italians, Etienne Turquet and Barthélemy Naris created silk industry in Lyons. At that time, France needed many skilled silk workers while there were many in surplus in Italy. These two Italian silk merchants got the authorization of French emperor to recruit skilled silk workers from Genoa to settle in Lyons with their families. Once settled in Lyons, they could enjoy the privilege of tax exemption on the condition that they had to work in Lyons all their lives. In 1537, the municipal government of Lyons was granted the monopoly for silk production by

Silk samples collected by Lyon Silk Museum in France.

The 1st volume of "the Quarterly Journal of Lyon Chinese French University," which use a silk pattern as its mark, states in its 1st editorial that the silk thread which knitted the pattern also linked closely between the Lyon Chamber of Commerce and China, a very important document in the studies on the Silk Road.

the king of France. Etienne Turquet and Barthélemy Naris organized Lyons Association of Silk Workshops. Although this was a private trust, it always cooperated with the city government and drew the first regulations for the silk industry and trade in 1554.

It was a time of rapidly development of textile industry. French textile industry not only satisfied the needs of its own country, but also made an inroad into the European market. Despite of numerous Italian migrants, France still felt the shortage of working force. In order to satisfy the demands in highly specialized workers, it had to train local

French workers. Therefore, some children in orphanages were sent to Lyons as apprentices. According to the classic Western division of labor, the types of work in the silk manufacturing industry were workman, workwoman and child labor. The division of labor in French workshop was as follows: workwoman engaged in spinning and rolling threads, workman engaged in weaving, and child labor engaged in auxiliary work. There were lots of families, whose members all were employed by spinning mills. Their jobs were succeeded from generation to generation and so were their skills. The swarming of workers brought about a housing crisis. Apart from building up multi-layer houses, the city of Lyons began to spread to suburbs. The textile mills couldn't support themselves in raw material supply and had to depend on the import of raw silk. Towards 19th century, France was the main client of Italian raw silk.

The silk industry of Europe was influenced by two factors. One was the ever-changing fashion; the other was the contradictions between the textile industry and the cocoon production, which was always lagging behind the demand of the textile industry.

In Europe, the alliance of countries were formed together and technological revolutions were taking place in one country after another, which benefited the textile industry a great deal. In 1605, major spinning machine was invented. It could not only raise production efficiency, but also weave exquisite silk fabrics with large patterns. In 1801, jacquard was invented, which could reduce half of the weavers. In 1860, the emergence of fuchsine dyestuff radically changed the printing and dyeing art. Various working procedures were improving year after year. The production cost was decreasing.

However, the process of cocoon production still remained at the stage of manual operation and limited to family production. Therefore, the output of raw silk couldn't satisfy the needs of textile industry. This problem wasn't resolved even in Lyons.

The changed life style had great impact on the silk industry of Europe. In 15th -16th centuries, people liked single-color woolen cloth. But in 17th century, people were fond of satin with prairie pattern, Turkey-type taffeta and fabrics with Milan-type pattern 18th century witnessed another vogue for large-scale patterns as well as costumes with patterns of fruits, trees, shells and fowl feathers. This was an idyllic time, extolled by Rousseau.

It was also a time that in Europe started to use Chinese patterns, such as Buddhist towers, bamboo bridges and figures. However, in 18th century, the pattern designers in Lyons were not familiar with fine Chinese traditions, such exquisite patterns in Song Dynasty, powerful patterns in Tang Dynasty and rigorous patterns in Han Dynasty. They only repeatedly copied and imitated the decadent arts in Qing Dynasty.

It was a time, when the East Indian Corporation was prospering, and Great Britain was rising at the heels of Holland. No matter how primitive were the Chinese patterns on the silk cloths, they reflected the increasing exchanges between Europe and the East. Ships, with full loads of Chinese porcelains and teas, set off inland rivers, first run to ports in Guangzhou or Fujian, then transmitted the cargo to motorized vessels for their final destinations in Europe. Chinese porcelains ended up in the parlors or drawing rooms in London, Paris and Amsterdam. After the silk, Chinese tea began to be a large item of commodities in the world. However, the Western World knew very little about the secret of Chinese tea production.

At the time of Chinese patterns decorating European costumes, there was another great event in the field of culture. In the ardent argument about propriety and righteousness, China's Confucian ideas permeated Catholic France. Lots of priests were invited to China as scholars. They gained excessive good favors in Chinese royal court. They actively preached and publicized Catholicism. However, in the course of preaching, they came across a hindrance. Chinese refused to give up their tradition of Confucian protocols.

In order to overcome the difficult, Catholic priests tried to make reconcile the two schools of thoughts. They said, Confucian ideas on propriety and righteousness weren't religious faith, but only non-religious code of behaviors. Therefore, Confucian ideas were compatible with Catholicism. The Vatican was very angry at this interpretation. The debate attracted many ideologists. People raised a lot of issues related to the essence of Confucianism. The West was more concerned about China. However, they were looking China from a Catholic perspective.

Later on, French philosopher Voltaire publicly admired Chinese political system. The missionaries sowed the seeds of Catholicism in China, but this exchange of culture was fragile and momentary. It had little impact on Chinese life in general.

As missionaries left China for home, Chinese porcelains, fans and other utensils were exported to Europe. But generally speaking China and Europe were still apart and did not really understand each other during that century. When opium trade led to war and British gunboats invaded Chinese waters, the East and the West cultures eventually collided.

There was once a crisis in French silk industry. Its market was flooded by cotton cloth with a variety of designs, sizes and colors, imported from Persia or India, which affected the silk industry in Lyons tremendously. From the beginning of 1800, a new feature was characteristic of the silk industry. Silk entered into the life of the common people. The silk production had to accommodate the needs of the ordinary people: less luxurious silk fabrics and more popular ones being manufactured. That was the first transformation of French silk industry.

From 19th century, because of the pressure to reduce production cost, silk merchants made efforts to get cheap raw silk and avoid the cost of long-distance trade in order to meet the demands for silk from the common people. However, the appearance of motor vessel affected the long distance trade. The operation of motor vessel greatly reduced the dangers along the sea route and shortened the time of navigation. The raw material in the Far East was also much cheaper. Therefore, the eyes of the Western silk businessmen turned to the coast of China and the silk trade between the East and the West prospered again.

The Interaction of Civilizations between the East and the West

China's Four Inventions and the Influence of the East

Papermaking, typography, fire powder and compass are four world-famous inventions of China, which were the symbol character-ized the ancient civilization and had played an important role in pro-moting the social development. Of the four inventions, compass was directly related with navigation. The West acquired the technology via sea route, while papermaking, typography and powder were considered to be introduced to the West along the Silk Road. This exchange had a great impact on the economy and culture of Europe and Asia.

Papermaking technology is invented by Chinese through a long his-tory of production practice. Before China invented paper, ancient Egypt wrote on papyrus, and the countries in southwestern Asia used wood block to write. Ancient Greece and Rome used papyrus imported from Egypt. In the Mediaeval Ages, Europe used sheepskin to write. In ear-lier times, China used bamboo slips, wooden tablets and silk cloths to record documents. Wooden tablet was heavy and cumbersome. Silk cloth was light but expensive. In early 2nd century, based on the experience accumulated from the generations of craftsmen, Cai Lun of the Eastern Han Dynasty succeeded in producing quality paper using fibres from linen, tree skin and broken fish net.

With the opening of the Silk Road, Chinese papers became important commodities, exported to the West via Xinjiang area. Stein discovered papers used by Sogdians, in the Great Wall relics in western Gansu. He estimated that the paper belonged to the middle period of the 2nd century. Moreover, he also discovered many pages of paper of official documents or private letters, in the ancient Lolan ruins, which were belonging to the last half of 2nd century. After 1949, Chinese archeologists discovered the earliest papers of Eastern Han Dynasty in Xinjiang when wooden tablets were still in general use. It was after the 2nd century that paper became the popular material to write. Afterwards, paper was introduced first to the Central Asia.

Although paper was used extensively in the Central Asia towards the end of the 5th century, China's papermaking technology was not introduced to this region until the middle period of the 8th century. Some Western scholars estimated that China's papermaking technology was introduced to the Central Asia around AD 704. However it is now generally acknowledged that AD 751 was an important year and that year Chinese papermaking technology was introduced to the Central Asia. According to the historic records of Tang Dynasty, in the July of 751, the general of Tang Dynasty Gao Xianzhi led Chinese army to fight Arabians in Talas and was defeated. Many soldiers were captured, and among them were craftsmen, locksmiths and papermaking workers. In 793, papermaking mills appeared in Persia. In 793-794, papermaking workshops were also established in Baghdad, Egypt, Morocco and several other countries. It was in the first half of the 12th century that Spain started to make papers. But the technology was still under the control of Arabians. In 1189, papermaking mills appeared in France. This is the earliest record of opening a workshop to make papers in a Christian country. Afterwards, papermaking technology reached Italy, Germany and Britain. Until the end of 18th century, paper ws made by hand Europe in the old fashioned Chinese tradition.

Typography is another great invention of China. Some scholars suggested that, engraving printing appeared in China as early as 6th century AD. But others disagree and believed a later date. However, both Chinese and foreign scholars agreed engraving printing emerged in China no later than 7th century. Chinese made a breakthrough in typography toward the middle period of 11th century. In that year, Bi Sheng invented the technique of interchangeable type sets which marked the beginning of a modern technology. Bi Sheng used baked clay types which were replaced by type sets made of tin and copper.

China's typography was gradual transferred to the West through the Silk Road. Scrolls of printed materials with images and letters were discovered in Dunhuang, Turpan and other places in Xinjiang. This indicated that engraving printing first arrived at Hexi and Xinjinag areas, and gradually traveled westward to Arabian areas. In 1880, in Egypt excavated large quantities of documents among which were 50 pieces of print work. Research indicated that, the print work dated from AD 900 to 1350. The print format and the method of printing were similar to that of China.

In 13th century, during the period of Yuan Dynasty, numerous travelers came to China via the Silk Road, seeing how Chinese printed books, paper currency and cards by engraving block and interchangeable typesets. And they brought these technologies back to Europe. In the 14th century, Europeans began to use engraving blocks. In the mid-15th century, they began to use interchangeable typesets. In 1466, Italy was the first to set up printing shops. From then on the technology was widely available in Europe.

Fire powder was invented by China. Alchemists first discovered natural material containing nitrate and sulfate and gradually they discovered that the two mix together and with they could make a fire power. China invented fire powder no later than Tang Dynasty. Afterwards, with the continual improvements of the technology to extract nitrate, fire powder could be used for military purpose. Toward the end of Tang Dynasty, "flying fire" of rockets was used in the battle fields. By the late North Song Dynasty, powerful cannon was used to fire ball of explosive against enemy.

Fire powder was first introduced to Arabia together with alchemy. Between 8th and 9th centuries, stones of nitrate, the most important raw material for fire powder was introduced to Arabia and it was called "Chinese Snow." They were used tot to make pills of immortality and also used in the glass making process. Toward 12th-13th centuries, Arabian merchants brought back from China the technology of making fire powder and fireworks on the Silk Road. After the 13th century, Mongolian army brought fire powder to the Central and Western Asia. In 1220, when Genghis Khan attacked Bukhara and Samarkand, he used artilleries and rockets. A great number of Chinese weapon craftmens arrived at the Central Asia. In the late 13th century, Europeans gained the knowledge of fire powder from Arabians. Toward the early 14th century, Europe acquired the technology to make gun power and used firearms in the war against Islamic countries. Hence Europe mastered the technology.

With the opening of the Silk Road, the cultural exchange between the East and the West became more frequent. Chinese culture continuously spread westwards. Chinese astronomy was well developed from ancient times. Chinese astronomers in Yuan Dynasty were invited to work at the Malagia Observatory in the present Azerbaijan.

In 8th and 9th centuries AD, Chinese medicine was reached Arabian regions with the development of alchemy. Medical Science, written by the famous Arabian medical scientist Avicenna discussed the technique of pulse examination. His method was very similar to that of Chinese medical science. In the late 16th century and the early 17th century, Matteo Ricci, Giulio Aleni and other Europeans arrived at China and they started to translate books of Chinese medicine into European languages. For the first time they introduced Chinese Compendium of Materia Medica to Europe.

It is worth to note that the Chinese paper manufacture and printing technology were introduced to the West as the advanced technologies and at the same time their introduction also showed Europe the excellent Chinese culture. Chinese paper manufacture and printing technology affected the Western culture and ideology a great deal and it is difficult to image how the European societies would have developed without their arrival?

At the same time when Chinese culture went to the West, other Asian and European cultures continuously came eastwards to China along the Silk Road which affected the development of China to a great extend. The followings played an important role in the transformation of Chinese societies since their arrival: acrobatics, dramas, music, dance and religion.

The Influence of the Western Cultures on Chinese Society

The Western acrobatics had long been introduced to China. This was recorded in Shi Ji (Records of the Grand Historian). In Han Dynasty, most of foreign acrobatics were performed in open squares. Their performances included various acts of fighting, boxing, athletics, masquerade, singing and dancing, contest with animals and magic.

In Tang Dynasty, and the culture exchanges between China and the West increased after the opening of the Silk Road. A variety of dramas, acrobatics and circuses from the Central Asia and the Western countries came to China. It was recorded that during the reign of Tang Xuanzong, the royal palace had hundreds of horses and trainers to train horses to dance.

In early Tang Dynasty, Polo ball game was introduced from Persia to China. It was a game to be played while riding on a horse. It was very popular with the royalties when in the royal palace prepared a special field for the game and a special pavilion was built for people to watch the game. Several emperors were reported to have mastered the game. The game was popular until the end of Ming Dynasty.

In Tang Dynasty, a game involving sprinkling water was also popular. It was invented in the Central Asia. People in both Chang'an and Luoyang liked the game very much and soon after even emperors began to play the game.

As early as when Zhang Qian traveled to the Western Regions, foreign music began to reach China. The music of Central Asia and India spread to China during After-Wei and Pre-Liang periods. The music of Samarkand was introduced to China when Wu Zetian was in power.

Several musical instruments were introduced to China from Persia and India. *Konghou* and lute were Persian musical instruments, introduced to China in Western Han Dynasty. Some argued that lute was originated in ancient India. However, all these musical instruments were improved and became part of traditional Chinese musical instruments.

In Tang Dynasty, there were exercise dance and soft dance or martial dance and culture dance. There were three kinds of exercise dance and they were *Huxuan* dance, *Huteng* dance and *Zhezhi* dance. All of them were introduced to China from the Central Asia.

Huxuan dance was originated in the Central Asian. According to the historic records, they repeatedly presented Huxuan dancing girls to Tang Dynasty. The famous poet of Tang Dynasty Bai Juyi vividly described the *Huxuan* dance:

Huxuan *girls,* Huxuan *girls,*

With beautiful costumes and long sleeves,

Dancing to the accompaniment of music.

Rotating now toward the left, now toward the right,

They danced like the snow flying.

Huteng dance were also originated in the Central Asia. It arrived in China in Tang Dynasty. Poet Li Duan gave a fine and detailed description of this dance:

The dancing girls wore light and gentle shirts,

With a long grape-like strips drooping down in front.

They knelt down before the emperor,

Thanked the rule in local accent.

And rolling up the sleeves and the shirts,

They danced gracefully and beautifully.

Raising their eyebrows and turning their eyes,

They swirled around on the colored tapestry.

Tired and sweating, reeling right and left, as if drunken,

They crossed their hands backward,

Just like the crescent moon in the sky.

Zhezhi dance was also originated in the Central Asia. Poet Liu Yuxi worte:

Dancing girls swirled to the accompaniment of drums;

Their waists are as soft as the drooping willows.

Sweats penetrate their silk clothes,

As if the drops of rain sprinkle on them.

Another poet Shen Yazhi wrote:

Dancing girls rock and roll

Like ducks swim in the pool.

Their eyes sweep around,
Full of love and affection.

It was clear that *Zhezhi* dance was full of graceful movements and facial expressions. The music and dances was introduced to China via the Silk Road and it was natural that they reached the border areas first where many Chinese minority nationalities lived. Therefore, the music and dances were and still are very popular in these areas and most of them are with musical talents. Today, Chinese music and dance are a very important national heritage and during its long history of development, many elements were originated in the neighboring countries and beyond.

Renaissance of the Silk Road and Dunhuang Buddhist Manuscripts

Sven Hedin

One day in May of 1895, in the wide and deep Taklamakan Desert, a weary-looking foreigner slowly but stubbornly crawled ahead. This was the Swedish explorer and archeologist Sven Hedin.

Toward the end of the 19th century, two academic hot topics were attracting the attention of the Western scientific community: geographic exploration and archeological investigation. The establishment of modern geographic science made aq group of scientist and explorers to investigate and conquer every untapped corner of the world. African exploration by Livingston and South Pole investigation by Scott and Amonsen made a sensation throughout the world. A great amount of valuable cultural relics, excavated from the site of ancient Troy city and Tutankamang Mausoleum promoted the birth of a fresh branch of science – archeology.

It was against such a background that Sven Hedin was brought up. At the age of 21, he traveled alone through Russia, Central Asia and

Persia. Afterwards, he was admitted to the Berlin University and received education from professor Lischhufen, the founder of modern geography. He was deeply moved by Lischhufen's experience of Asian exploration and his story of what he had seen and heard along the Silk Road. Sven Hedin determined to go to Turkestan (the present Xinjiang in China) and to explore this strange, desolate and mysterious land.

In February 1895, Sven Hedin traveled through frigid temperature and atrocious weather and over Pamirs and arrived at Kashgar. According to local legend, lots of ancient cities were buried in the depths of Taklamakan Desert; and everywhere there were rare and valuable treasures, which were protected and defended by devils. Those, who searched for such treasures, seldom came back alive. Sven Hedin was intrigued by the legend. He went to Merket from Kashgar, bought 8 camels and stocked enough provisions for one month, recruited 3 guides, and set out for Taklamakan Desert exploration in April 1895. The villagers, who saw him off, shook their heads and said, "He would possibly never return."

As expected after 15 days traveling in the desert, they had drinking water only enough for 2 days. The desert was endless and no edge was in

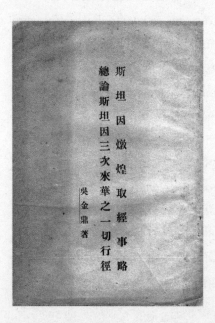

How Stein Acquired Dunhuang Buddhist Scriptures, *by Wu Jinding.*

sight. If turned back, it might be possible for them to return along the same route. But Sven Hedin decided to go ahead continually. He reduced the ration of water for everyone and gave no water to camels. At night, they dug ground to search for water, but hardly they had any luck. Next day, desert storm attacked them. Sven Hedin had no choice but to discard 2 sick camels and baggages. At this critical moment, a guide stealthily drunk up the last drops of water. Angry companions nearly beat him to death. Sven Hedin reckoned this was the end for him. He despairingly wrote his last diary.

On May 4th, the 5th day, Sven Hedin still stubbornly wrestled with death. The servants all exhausted, with lips dry and cracked, lying motionless on sand. Only Sven Hedin still crawled forth with his last company. When the sun was rising, Sven Hedin surprised to find a clear pond of water. He began to drink the water greedily. His pulse recovered its normal beating. His dry skin became moist again. The first exploration ended in a failure, with the death of 2 men and the lost of all mapping instruments. The life and death struggle constituted a most breath-taking chapter in his book Safari in Asian Hinterland. However, this hardship didn't shake his resolve to continue his exploration.

In late 1895, Sven Hedin and his entourage again set out from Kashgar to Yutian along the southern section of the Silk Road. He purchased a lot of excavated cultural relics and ancient document manuscripts from villagers all the way. It was a pity that Sven Hedin had only a very limited archeological knowledge. His purpose was to discover ancient cities in the desert. From Hotan, they walked eastward for more than ten days. Sven Hedin found at last the ruins of two small ancient cities. He was pleasantly surprised to discover ancient houses, trees and Buddhism frescos and sculptures. On the walls of an ancient temple, he set eyes on the figures of many women. Their black hairs coiled up on their heads. Their eyebrows were long and thin. There were auspicious moles on their forehead. It was undoubtedly belonging to Indian Buddhism arts.

Sven Hedin also explored the southern Xinjiang and drew a lot of maps. Afterwards, he entered the mysterious Tibet. When he concluded his second exploration and returned to Sweden, he received a warm red-carpet welcome.

The greatest achievement of Sven Hedin was his third exploration in Taklamakan Desert in September 1899. Under the auspices of Swedish king Oscar and scientist Alfred Bernhard Nobel, he led an exploration team to investigate the Yarkant River and Charkhlik before going to Lop Nor at the furthest eastern end of the desert.

One day in late September 1899, they stayed overnight at an ancient site and hurried on with their journey next morning. Unexpectedly, a servant lost the only shovel on the camping ground. Sven Hedin ordered him going back to find it. The servant returned with the shovel and several beautiful woodcarvings, which made Sven Hedin very excited. He intended to hurry back to excavate the site. But the drinking water was in short supply. He dared not run the risk again. He wasn't aware that this accidental discovery would bring him the climax for his exploration life.

Next winter, Sven Hedin returned to Lop Nor and made excavations at the ancient site for 7 days. The greatest achievement this time was the discovery of parcels of ancient documents and wooden slips in Chinese. Back in Sweden, he handed the cultural relics to a Sinologist for appraisal. It was confirmed that Sven Hedin discovered Lolan – an ancient country of the Western Regions on the Silk Road in Han Dynesty. According to Shi Ji, in Han Dynasty, Lolan was a communication center on the Silk Road. As a transfer station for China, Persia, India as well as the West World, Lolan was the place, where the silk and tea of China's Central Plains and the excellent horses, jewelries and other special local products of the Western Regions were swapped.

Because of its strategic importance, this small town of 14,000 residents boasted of 3,000 Chinese army. In order to flight for the control

敦煌石室古卷軸西航者歸英法東漸者歸日本我國搜其餘
尚得數千卷予既一一披覽之又影寫歸法京之古經籍數十
種而英倫與日本所得則不獲寫焉今年夏至武庫觀西陲
古物展覽會始與親至石室之橘氏 相見亟請觀所得經
卷慨然見其經名則據原題錄之其最先者始元魏後者訖五季其
尾題印記其經名則許其目示以編目中所列凡四百餘軸詳記其第
秩然有條理焉今藏經目備覽之而以今藏校其異同存佚頗
大經印蓋合諸伽藍所藏併入石室於是可窺見西域當時象
印記有報恩寺藏經印淨土寺藏經印三界寺藏經印瓜沙州
教之興盛也其經文橘氏已校勘將次第印入二樂叢書而題

記中可考證史事者不少因請假是目以歸簫燈錄之將印行
以詒當世噫石室卷軸入歐洲者其卷數不可知然約計先後
所出當不下二萬軸予獲觀者三之一耳其已編目者若我學
部所得五六千卷雖草艸而未寫定今且存亡未可知法京則
編目而未印行英國開尚未遑編寫其寫定可印行者此卷而
已然則橘氏編定之功烏可泯而不傳與惟橘氏所得尚未盡
列目中予所見尚有晉元康所寫法華經等又繼橘氏而往之
吉川氏小一郎所擄歸尚百餘卷亦未編錄今先印是卷他日
所編當請而續印之是書卷端以誌欣慨時甲寅八月二十八
日上虞羅振玉書於東山寓居之大雲精舍

橘序

一

經部　總三百六十七卷

妙法蓮華經卷一
又卷第二　以後顋西天取經僧繼從乾德六年二月日科記
　　　　　上二卷貞元錄卷二十八云係鵠經
又卷第三
又卷第四
又卷第五
又卷第六

日本橘氏敦煌將來藏經目錄

The list of Buddhist manuscripts complied by Japanese Dunhuang scholars illustrated in the book entitled *Xue Tang Cong Ke* by Luo Zhengyu in 1914.

over the Western Regions, wars broke out many times between China and Hun in Lolan. In 77 BC the general of Han Dynasty Huo Guang assassinated the king of Lolan because of his Hunophile position and planted a new pro-Han Emperor. Its capital moved southward and re-named Shanshan. In early AD 6th century, Lolan was still thriving and prospering. But afterwards Lolan gradually disappeared from the scene. Now it appeared again before the world. That was the reason why the Swedish explorer became so excited.

When Sven Hedin was making excavations in the Lolan site, another European explorer and archeologist Marc Aurel Stein began the first venture of his three large-scale investigations along the Silk Road at the other end of the Taklamakan Desert.

Renaissance of the Silk Road and Dunhuang Buddhist Manuscripts

165

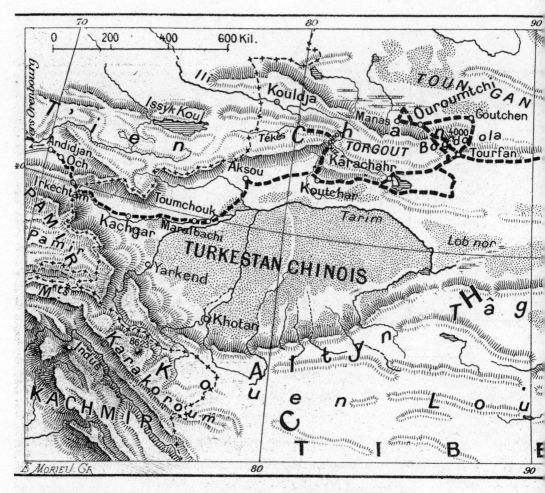

A map showing the expedition of six thousand kilometers through Turkistan and China by Paul Pelliot and his team.

Marc Aurel Stein

Marc Aurel Stein was a Jew, born in Hungary. As a young man, he studied Oriental languages and archeology in Europe. Later on, he went to India working for the British. When he read *Safari in Asian Hinterland* by Sven Hedin, he was very excited and he made up his mind to search for treasures along the Silk Road. He applied to the British colonial authorities in India for passport and funds, and received the due support.

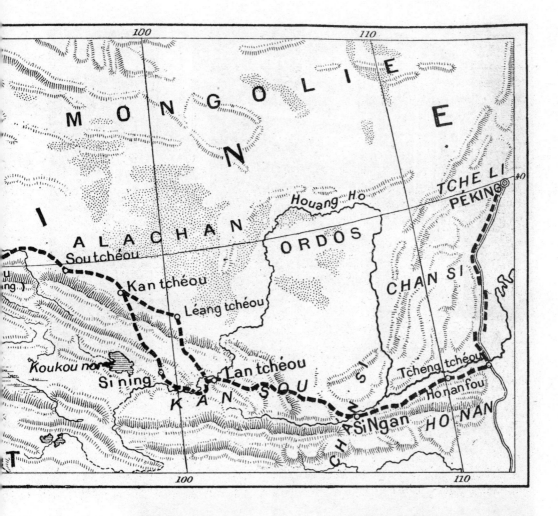

Paul Pelliot and his key team members.

The Paul Pelliot room at Museum Louvre, most of collections coming from China.

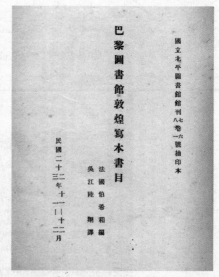

巴黎圖書館敦煌寫本書目

國立北平圖書館館刊八七卷六一號抽印本

法國伯希和編
吳江陸翔譯

民國二十三年十一二十二月

The list of Dunhuang manuscripts at Paris Library. *Dunhuang manuscripts have been brought to and kept in England, Japan and France with France collecting the most copies.*

Paul Pelliot kept account of fifteen thousand copies of manuscripts in Dunhuang caves.

In May 1900, an exploration team, composed of Stein and his 4 assistants, started from Kashmir, crossed Karakorum Mountains and arrived in Kashgar. They continued the journey toward Hotan along the southern edge of Taklamakan Desert. When he first set foot in the desert, Stein wrote, "The desert stretched faraway to the distant south like a boundless ocean, because the sand dunes looks like sea waves. The dunes rise higher and higher. It is more and more difficult to crawl over them. The hoofs of the short horses sunk deep in the friable and loose sands. The crawling up of 3-40 inches makes us perspiring and sweating profusely." Occasionally they came across a small oasis, but in most cases they were trudged in desolate and uninhabited land.

After arrived in Hotan, Stein began to search for treasures everywhere. He aimed at finding ancient documents and artworks. Under the guidance of the local people, he recruited 30 workers and walked for 11 days in the northeast direction of Hotan, and at last arrived at Dandan Oylik – an ancient site in the depth of Taklamakan Desert. Here Stein found plenty of frescos, sculptures and documents in Turki and Chinese. Among the documents there were two certificates of debt, dated Jianzhong 3 (c. AD 782), which confirmed most of the documents belonged to Tang Dynasty.

The discovery of 3 board paintings made Stein especially excited. One of them painted a warrior, riding a horse. His young face was characteristic of the mixed Sino-Indian features, with black long hairs coiled up on his head. He wore a pair of black boots with felt linings. His waist hung a Persia-styled long sword. This picture skillfully melted the influences from China, India and Persia into one, which reflected the cultural exchanges along the Silk Road in the 7th century.

After boxing up the hundreds of cultural relics, excavated in Dandan Oilyk, Stein went further to Niya (in the present northern-eastern of Minfeng County, Xinjiang). In Niya, he found plenty of wooden slips and documents, most of them belonging to Han and Jin dynasties. There were also some wooden slips, written in ancient Indian language with clay seals. He was surprised to discover that on the wooden slips were painted the images of Greek goddess Athena and other gods in the style of Western classic paintings. It was clear that in the West Jin Dynasty, the Western arts had already spread to the Western Regions along the Silk Road.

In May 1901, Stein concluded his first exploration and returned to Britain with 12 boxes full of valuable cultural relics. The archeological achievements of Stein made sensation throughout Europe. And he successfully gained enough funds for his second exploration. In 1907, Stein crossed the Pamirs Plateau and arrived in Kashgar and began his second exploration. Because he didn't know Chinese, he recruited a Chinese teacher Jiang Xiaowan to assist him.

This time his destination was Lolan. He recruited 50 persons, ten times the number Sven Hedin had in his team to Lolan. Under the guidance of Sven Hedin's map, he successfully reached Lolan. In terms of archeology, he was much more proficient and informative than Sven Hedin. He found plenty of ancient documents of Han Dynasty and ancient wooden slips of India, which indicated, when Chinese withdrew from the Western Regions in Wei and Jin dynasties, Indians once lived there. He also unexpectedly found the metal tape Sven Hedin lost there in 1901. Afterwards, at a London banquet, he returned the tape to Sven Hedin.

Stein left Lolan for an ancient site called Miran in the Lop Nor. In a ruined temple, he was surprised to discover plenty of exquisite Western-styled frescos. On one of the frescos painted a winged angel. Another fresco had the sign of Titus – Roman emperor in AD 79. It seemed that in Han Dynasty a Rome artist or one, who had learned classic Roman painting, had come to the city on the edge of Lop Nor.

After taken off these valuable frescos from the cave walls, Stein marched toward Dunhuang in February 1907. At that time, Dunhuang had long lost its prosperity of Tang Dynasty and became a small desolate and obscure town. Stein originally planned to replenish provisions in Dunhuang and to return to Lolan immediately. In the hostel, he talked with other travelers. It was said that in Mogao Caves were discovered a great amount of ancient documents, which intrigued him at once. He decided to go to there. This decision resulted in the most astonishing discovery of cultural relics along the Silk Road in the 20th century.

Several years ago, a poor Taoist priest Wang Yuanlu came to the Mogao Caves to live. One day, when he knocked at the walls, he discovered an empty cave. He removed the wall of the cave and saw a small chamber, full of hand-copied Scriptures and documents. Semiliterate, Wang Yuanlu didn't know their value. So he sent several volumes to the officials of Dunhuang and Gansu for appraisal. Although these officials of Qing Dynasty were aware of the value of these ancient documents, they had no idea about what to do. They only told the Taoist priest to seal off the wall. However, the message was spreading quickly. When Stein heard the story he went there immediately.

When Stein met with the Taoist priest Wang Yuanlu however, he was tight-mouthed and never said a single word about the Chamber. Stein didn't know what to do. He had no choice but to pretend as an investigating tourist. After consulting his Chinese teacher Jiang, Stein told Taoist priest Wang, he was a lover of Buddhism artworks; he intended to donate some funds to help repair Mogao Caves; in order to work out a plan of repairing, he hoped to look around all the caves. On hearing this, priest Wang readily consented and served as a guide. Faced with so many exquisite frescos and sculptures, Stein became more and more excited. He told priest Wang, he came from India, heard the story of how Xuanzang experienced hardships and dangers for acquiring Buddhism Scriptures from India, and that was why he respected Xuanzang. Priest Wang was very moved by the sweet words of Stein and treated him as a good friend. In the afternoon next day, priest Wang opened the wall of the Chamber. Under the dim light of an oil lamp, Stein bending his head, crawled into the cave-like chamber.

They worked round the clock. Every day priest Wang carried out a batch of documents for Stein and Teacher Jiang to select. The documents were so numerous and colorful. There were not only hand-copied Buddhist scriptures, but also paintings, letters as well as account books and certificates of debt. Most of them were belonging to Tang Dynasty. Thanks to the dry weather in Dunhuang, Most documents were kept intact. According to the estimate of Stein, the total of documents numbered no less than 50,000. Apart from documents in Chinese, there were manuscripts in Sanskrit, Kangjuese, ancient Tibetan, ancient Uighur and other languages. Stein didn't know Chinese, and Jiang had very limited knowledge in this field, so that it was difficult for them to ascertain which document was more valuable. However, Stein as the first reader who took away plenty of valuable documents. For instance, one volume of xylographic Vajracchedika-sutra, dated Tang Xiantong 9th (AD 868), was the most ancient printed work discovered so far in the world. At the first page of the clearly printed volume was a fine illustration of numerous Buddha images.

After having read lots of documents, Stein got to understand the history of the Chamber. In the prosperous period of Tang Dynasty, Mogao Caves was a Buddhism Holy Land on the Silk Road and an exchange center for various branches of Buddhism school in India, ancient Tibet and the Western Regions. There was a rich collection of Scriptures.

When Tang Wuzong was in power, he banned Buddhism. Temples throughout the country were damaged. At that time, Dunhuang was under the control of ancient Tibet. That was why it survived the purge. In the period of "Five Dynasty," owing to chaos caused by wars and natural disasters, the priests and monks in the Mogao Caves were forced to run away. Before leaving, they stored Buddhist Scriptures into a secret Chamber. The monks went and never returned. And the Chamber became a secret place nobody knew its existence. Scriptures slept there for more than one thousand years.

Stein took away 6,000 titles of documents as well as numerous fine artworks, such as Buddhist streamers and embroideries. He packed them into 29 large wooden boxes, transported by camels. 16 months later, he arrived in London.

Stein satisfactorily said good-bye to priest Wang and gave him 500 *liang* (a unit of weight, equal to 50 grams) silver as donation. Priest Wang was very grateful, because he never saw so great a sum of funds in all his life. However, when he crossed the Pamirs, Stein's two feet were frostbitten. He endured bitter pains and rode camel, continually marching onward. In a small city in Afghan, he underwent a surgical operation. A British church doctor operated on the gangrenous toes of his right foot.

In 1914, Stein came to China for his third archeological research. He once more went to Mogao Caves. After bargaining, he again took away 500 volumes of hand-copied sutras of Tang Dynasty from priest Wang.

Stein returned to Britain as a triumphant hero. The king of Britain awarded him a Knighthood. Oxford and Cambridge Universities made him an honorary doctor of philosophy. The most exciting of all was he acquired British nationality. The great amount of art treasures and his books on the exploration experiences created much excitement in European archeological community. A greater wave of explorers followed his steps and came to China's Western Regions.

Paul Pelliot

One day in late August 1906, French Sinologist Paul Pelliot at the age of 27 years old traveled for more than two months and arrived at

Kashgar He knew he came too late. Explorers and archeologists from Britain, Sweden, Germany, Russia and Japan had been there many times.

But Paul Pelliot was not discouraged. He was a gifted linguist and spoke 13 languages. During the period of Yihetuan Movement (or Boxer Uprising) in 1900, he worked for the French embassy in Beijing. He was well aware of Chinese society and its history. This experience was very favorite to his exploration in China.

As soon as he was in Kashgar, he immediately visited Chinese officials and asked for favor and assistance. The bureaucrats of Qing Dynasty were surprised at the fact that this foreigner not only spoke fluent Chinese, but also was able to read aloud the couplets, hung on the walls of the drawing room. Paul Pelliot easily established friendly relations with these officials and got more special treatments than other foreigners.

When Stein was in Dunhuang and took away plenty of Mogao Caves treasures, Paul Pelliot knew nothing about it. One day, he met an aristocrat of Qing Dynasty in Urumqi. The latter handed him a piece of hand-copied sutra for appraisal and told him, there were lots of such sutras in Dunhuang Thousand-Boddha Caves, the Caves of Thousand Buddhas. He glanced at it and knew this was a valuable document of Tang Dynasty. He left for Dunhuang at once.

In March 1908, Paul Pelliot met priest Wang in Dunhuang. Thanks to his fluent Chinese and profound knowledge, he became a friend of priest Wang. The priest opened the wooden gate of the sutra cave. Paul Pelliot swept his eyes around under the dim light of wax candle and was stricken dumb with amazement. There remained at least 20,000 bundles of documents. He decided to browse through one by one. He worked night and day. After more than 20 days and nights, Paul Pelliot selected more than 600 volumes of valuable documents. He paid priest Wang 500 *liang* silver and wrote a guarantee of secrecy. When Paul Pelliot was selecting documents, his two assistants took pictures of hundreds of frescos and sculptures. However, Paul Pelliot didn't keep secret. After the documents were transported to France, he made known his discovery and showed some valuable documents in Beijing. Chinese scholars were astonished and asked the authorities to protect Chinese treasures. It was under these circumstances that the government of Qing Dynasty sealed off Dunhuang Thousand-Boddha Caves, the Caves of Thousand Buddhas, and transported all the remaining documents to Beijing.

In the period of more than 30 years from the late 19th century to the early 20th century, there were dozens of foreigners from Britain, Sweden, Japan, Russia, Germany and the United States coming to western China to explore the cultural sites on the Silk Road. On the one hand, they carried away great amounts of Dunhuang cultural relics and ancient documents, causing gigantic damages to Chinese culture. On the other hand, they enhanced the awareness of the importance of the Silk Road to the trade and cultural exchanges in ancient times, thus speeding up the recovery of the Silk Road.

In 1930s, When Sven Hedin investigated the Silk Road in the northern-western part of China, he wrote a memorandum to the Nanjing government, emphasizing the importance of recovering this ancient royal courier road, "Chinese silk had been continuously transported to the Western World for years. We are now in this desolate land, because we are studying how to recover this once very prosperous route linking Chinese backland and Asian hinterland, and how to improve it so that it adapts to the massive motor-driven vehicle traffic."

It was pity that since the World War II, due to various contradictions, the Silk Road was neglected for a long time and hadn't played the role as a bearer of exchanges between the East and the West.

It is until the late 20th century that with the recognition of the importance of the ancient trade and commercial road, the countries along the route strengthened the construction of traffic and transportation facilities. In September 1990, China's Lanzhou-Xinjiang railway extended to Allah Mountain Pass in Xinjiang, and linked with the railway of

Kazakhstan, thus forming a grand railway artery from China's Lianyungang in the east, westward through Kazakhstan, Russia, Ukraine, Poland, Germany, finally to Rotterdam in Holland. This 10,800-kilometer railway is the second Asian-European continental bridge besides the Siberian railway. Its distance of 2,000 kilometers was shorter than the Siberian railway. At the east end of this pan Asian-European continental bridge is the West-Pacific region with a strong economic growth. At its west end is the highly developed European Union. In the middle are the Central Asian and East-European regions, comparatively under developed but rich in resources. The three regions are economically complementary to each other. If they strengthen their cooperation, they certainly can achieve a common development and prosperity for each of their economies.

A brand-new era of international trade and commerce is coming to the old but glorious Silk Road. A modern flow of logistics, knowledge and resources will replace the primitive camel trade caravan of the past. This is a period of renaissance for the ancient Silk Road.